Swasti Mitter

Common Fate,
Common Bond

Women in the Global Economy

Pluto Press

First published in 1986 by Pluto Press Limited,
The Works, 105a Torriano Avenue, London NW5 2RX
and Pluto Press Australia Limited, PO Box 199, Leichhardt,
New South Wales 2040, Australia. Also Pluto Press,
27 South Main Street, Wolfeboro, New Hampshire, 03894-2069 USA

7 6 5 4 3 2 1

90 89 88 87 86

Set by Rapidset and Design Limited, London WC1

Printed in Great Britain by Cox & Wyman Ltd, Reading, Berks

British Library Cataloguing in Publication Data

Mitter, Swasti
  Common fate, common bond: women in the
  global economy.
1. Women — Employment   2. Work
environment
I. Title
331.4'2   HD6053

ISBN 0 7453 0026 X

Swasti Mitter was born in a small town in West Bengal, India. Since 1963 she has been living in England, which she has adopted as her country. Educated in Calcutta, the London School of Economics and Cambridge University, she is at present a senior lecturer in the Department of Business Management at Brighton Polytechnic. Her recent research focuses on the impact of new technology and multinationals on the gender structure of employment. She is married with two children.

Her *Peasant Movements in West Bengal* was published by the Department of Land Economy at Cambridge University.

Contents

To my dear beloveds and to women working worldwide

Abbreviations

AES	The Alternative Economic Strategy (of the Euro-Socialists)
ARTEP	Asian Regional Team for Employment Promotion
BIP	The Border Industrialization Programme (of Mexico)
EOI	Export-Oriented Industrialization
EPZ	Export Processing Zones, often called Free Trade Zones
FMS	Flexible Manufacturing System
ILO	International Labour Organization
IS	Import Substitution Policy
LIS	The London Industrial Strategy 1985
NT	New Technology
OECD	Organization for Economic Co-operation and Development (an economic block representing 24 countries including US, Western Europe, Turkey, New Zealand, Australia and Japan)
TNCs	Transnational Corporations
UNCTAD	United Nations Commission on Trade, Aid and Development

Preface

The subject of women in the global economy is not a new one. The central role of women workers in the current industrial restructuring has been stressed in a growing body of literature, particularly in the context of discussions of multinational corporations, since the mid-1970s. I was stimulated by these discussions to look at the world from a different perspective, and I acknowledge my debt to some of them in a select bibliography at the end of this book.

The major contribution of these studies has been to evoke a powerful and persistent image of the workers in the global factory. It is an image of young non-European women, who are engaged in low-paid, insecure, assembly-line jobs in the so-called 'Third World'. The image is particularly startling as it relates to traditional societies, where male unemployment is high and where women are not generally encouraged to take up factory work.

The strength of this image, however, has tended to obscure some fundamental underlying problems. What has been largely ignored till now is that the recruitment of insecure and disposable labour is not confined to underdeveloped countries. The creation of a new proletariat is in fact part of a wider management strategy that affects not only the Third World but also the First. It is a strategy that deliberately seeks a 'flexible' workforce in order to undermine the power of organized labour. The patriarchal values of the state and the family place women in a position of subjugation in the North as well as the South; hence it is in women everywhere that the large corporations find the promise of compliant labour. This is especially so as the male-dominated labour movement in all societies tends to marginalize the issue of women workers.

The casualization of employment is not confined to the global factories of the Third World. The phenomenal rise of home-based part-time and temporary work in the West is a manifestation of the same changed management practices. 'Flexible manning' is the order of the day, and this policy favours the enlisting of women workers. The trend accelerates as new technology makes fresh onslaughts on the traditionally male craft-skills.

One of the important consequences of new technology has been the ability of manufacturers to fragment the production processes into separate elements. This allows transnational corporations to shift the labour-intensive parts of production to far-away countries where there is an abundance of cheap female labour. But the same fragmentation allows large manufacturers to shift work to small subcontractors in the First World – for smaller units can avoid problems with unions and employment legislation with greater ease.

In some specific industries in the West, it is black women, in their home-based units, who offer the most flexible labour of all. In contrast, men – generally white men – retain their monopoly over a small number of elite 'core' jobs. The profitability of mobile international capital thus thrives on the politics of race and gender.

The creation of a largely female marginalized workforce has depended on the generally perceived role of women in the home and in society. Women's experience of marginalization, however, has also been instrumental in fostering a common bond: the resultant international networks of women workers are now seriously challenging the policies of international capital. In the process, they are providing powerful forums for questioning the accepted male visions of the labour movement, of growth and of development.

In this book I try to analyse both the background and the current manifestations of the struggle of women workers, as they attempt to change their fate in a world that is still dominated by the power of the global corporations.

Space does not allow me to mention the names of all the friends and colleagues who have helped and inspired me to write this book. Among them, some have played a decisive role in showing me how to look at the world economy from a woman worker's point of view. Anneke Van Luijken and I wrote an article together on homeworking in 1983; exploring the differences and similarities in the experiences of homeworkers in England, Holland and the Philippines made me aware for the first time of another dimension, one generally ignored, in the current industrial restructuring. Helen Allison and Gerry Reardon, Julia Burdett, Annie Ralph and many other friends from both Women Working Worldwide and the National Homeworking Group have been a constant source of support. So was Georgina Ashworth of Change.

I have learnt a great deal from Ursula Huws and Ruth Pearson in the last three years. Both have helped me with information, analysis and generous introductions to people and organizations. In the spirit of friendship they have carefully read this book in manuscript. Their comments have improved its content; its limitations are still mine. It was a pleasure to have Richard Kuper as editor at the Pluto Press. His gentle patience was deeply appreciated.

Valerie Chitty, Carolyn Gosling, and Cathy Newson transformed my illegible handwriting as if by magic into typed pages: my special thanks to them for their forbearance.

I always feel grateful to Partha, Rana and Pamina for their love. It is because of them that I have a lively and loving home where everything is shared, including domestic chores, with joy and without bitterness. Finally, my love and gratitude to Peter Dronke for all his encouragement and assistance. Without his help in editing and correcting the form and the content, this book would never have seen the light of day.

Swasti Mitter

1. Women and the changing structure of employment

Introduction

My awareness of the central role of women in the changing international division of labour began, significantly, in Brick Lane in the East End of London. It was the summer of 1982, and I was given leave from my polytechnic to do research on the impact of the recession and of technological changes on the immigrant communities, especially in the inner-city areas of London. Being myself a Bengali immigrant, albeit a privileged one, I ventured to start my investigation with the Bangladeshi community in the East End. There, in Tower Hamlets alone, nearly 60,000 Bangladeshi men, women and children have been relying on the 'rag trade' for their livelihood in the last two decades, having arrived in Britain during the post-war wave of immigration. As the recession hit hard, a large number of clothing factories, however rudimentary, closed their doors, pushing the level of unemployment among the male members of this community to an intolerable level. The response was one of near-panic in a community which had always prided itself on its self-reliance.

My visits to Bangladeshi families in 1982 opened up a new area of experience to me. While the jobs disappeared from garment factories, depriving white working-class women and immigrant men of work, the supply of machining work to female Bangladeshi homeworkers was on the increase. In many families it was the women who became the sole breadwinners. Women's increased earning potential shifted, even if only slightly, the balance of power between men and women, notwithstanding the oppressiveness of the male concept of 'Ijjat' (honour) in this deeply Islamic society.

The changing structure of employment between men and women, between blacks and whites, between factory work and homework, between the regulated and the unregulated economy, as manifested in the East End of London in the summer of 1982, appeared rather curious at the time. It took me a while to realize that what was happening in the East End was part of a wider restructuring in the rest of the industrializing and industrialized world. The visible shifts in the labour market were the outcome of a changed management strategy that aimed to nullify the rights and privileges that organized labour had won, especially in the West, through years of struggle.

The outcome of the new strategy has been the massive integration of blacks and women – and in many sectors black women workers – into the global economy in a new way. These workers are precisely the ones who have so far been marginalized in the mainstream labour movement. Their very vulnerability has made them a preferred labour force in an evolving pattern of business organization that tends to rely on flexible and disposable workers. The transnational corporations (TNCs), with their immense resources, engineer access to such workers by restructuring labour nationally as well as globally on the basis of race and gender. Colour and sex have thus become the main principles behind the most recent international division of labour.

The global division of labour

The older division of labour was the product of colonialism, under which it was the European countries – 'mother countries' as they were called – that provided manufactured goods in the world economy. The 'children' of the empires, on the other hand, were expected to provide the raw materials. This division of labour was not by any means a negotiated one and was imposed with an iron hand by the mother countries on the subject colonies. The emerging order was legitimized by articulated economic theories, such as that of David Ricardo in 1817, proposing that there were reciprocal benefits in international specialization. This theory was a glorification of free trade, and was a logical extension of Adam Smith's theory of the division of labour in 1776, that espoused the potential of improved efficiency through specialization at factory level.

As the relations of exchange were unequal, it was not surprising that the fruits of the colonial division of labour were mainly appropriated by the mother countries. As Marx noted in 1848 in *Discourse on Free Trade*:

> We are told, for example, that free trade will give rise to an international division of labour that will assign each country a production that is in harmony with its natural advantages. You may think, gentlemen, that the production of coffee and sugar is the natural destiny of the West Indies. Two centuries earlier, nature, which is unaware of commerce, had not placed either coffee trees nor sugar cane there . . . If the free traders cannot understand how one country can enrich itself at the expense of another, we should not be surprised, since these same gentlemen do not want to understand either that within a country one class can enrich itself at the expense of another.

The scope of this old division of labour gradually diminished with the independence of former colonial territories from 1947 onwards. Since many of the newly independent countries resorted to a policy of producing goods they formerly imported – a policy known as import-substitution (IS) – as a prudent way of developing their own industrial base, most Western-based large organizations found it problematic to retain or expand their markets in these countries. The import-substitution policy also implied a strict control of foreign exchange, thus curbing the profit repatriation of foreign companies. They also feared nationalization by the host governments.

The IS policy in the new countries often foundered for a number of reasons, such as the technological gap between them and the advanced countries, or acute difficulties regarding foreign exchange. In this scenario, an alternative model of growth captured the imagination of a number of the former colonies, particularly from the late 1960s onwards. The growth was to be spearheaded by exports, where investments by the transnational companies were to provide the necessary foreign exchange and technical expertise. The model of export-oriented industrialization (EOI) received the blessing of international agencies such as the International Monetary Fund (IMF) and the World Bank. In this model these agencies saw the possibility of an ideal division of labour. The non-European countries, lumped together in an undifferentiated category as 'Third World', would provide cheap labour, and the 'First World' would provide the capital. This new international division of labour, like the old, perpetuated the glory of specialization: each bloc according to its own ability!

The new order had yet another dimension: there was to be an increase in managerial control following from revolutionary technological changes. In fact, the shifting of the labour-intensive assembly-line operations to far-away countries was possible only because of spectacular changes in communication, transport and production technology. 'From Santa Clara in the US,' one of the managers of a transnational company claimed, 'Malaysia is only a telex away.' The introduction of computer and satellite technology opened up new possibilities of supervising production, which could then be dispersed globally. The scope of distributing production over a wide area also increased because the new technology made it possible to separate different elements of production effectively. This separation allowed managers to shift a sizeable part of assembly-line work either to far-away cheap labour countries or to smaller subcontractors at home. Either move reduced the power of organized labour. The large corporations, on the other hand, retained firm control over the knowledge-intensive part of production and, most of all, over retail outlets. In fact, the centralization of market and technology, together with the decentralization of production, have turned out to be the major features of the new international division of labour.

The expression 'the new international division of labour'[1] is more commonly used in a narrower sense than the one I have outlined. Its usage connotes a changing structure of employment, globally, through relocation of jobs from the high-wage countries of the West to low-wage, newly industrializing countries of Asia and Latin America. The expression has become common currency in discussions of the industrial restructuring of the mature capitalist countries; it is invariably used in debates concerning North–South dialogue. The introduction of the expression has above all helped to highlight the spectacular speed of the internationalization of capital, and the directions this has taken, from the late 1960s onwards. As more and more countries are integrated into the expanding empires of the late twentieth-century form of international business and capital, the workers of a nation-state become vulnerable to the investment and pro-curement policies of the TNCs. Even the government of a rich country can have only a limited influence over the decision-making processes of these giant corporations.

The volatile nature of TNC investment invariably means that the jobs in one country or power bloc are gained at the expense of jobs in another. This explains why, in the 12-year period between 1971 and 1983, when 1.5 million workers, mostly women, lost their jobs in the clothing and textiles industry in Europe and the United States, two million or more women workers found jobs in the clothing and textile industry in the Third World.[2] Even in the sunrise industries, such as electronics, the relocation of jobs to low-wage countries has been high. Whereas knowledge-intensive aspects of work remained in the US's Silicon Valley or in Japan, assembly and other labour-intensive operations were repeatedly shifted to countries with cheaper labour costs, in Latin America and Asia.

The ensuing changes in trade relationships between the mature advanced capitalist countries and the newly emerging economies have turned particularly on the electronics, clothing and textile industries. In spite of the hysteria that has arisen around the shifting structure of employment in favour of the so-called (undifferentiated) Third World, the share of 122 countries (lumped together as 'the South') in overall world trade changed only marginally in the course of the 1970s. Even in the late 1970s, Third World countries contributed only 8 to 10 per cent of the world's manufacturing trade and about 1 per cent of the Western market for final goods. The much publicized redistribution of employment and industrial capacity, resulting from the new in-ternational division of labour, has favoured only a handful of in-dustrializing countries in the South – four in East Asia (South Korea, Hong Kong, Taiwan and Singapore), and two in Latin America (Mexico and Brazil). There were other newly in-

dustrializing countries, such as India, that were uncertain about
the desirability of being linked to international capitalism, and
still others, such as Yugoslavia, that were not unambiguously of
the 'Third World'. From the 1970s more non-European countries, however, began to join the ranks of those linked to international capital: Malaysia, Thailand, the Philippines, Ven-
ezuela, Indonesia, Egypt, Sri Lanka, Bangladesh and, after
some political changes, the People's Republic of China.[3]

Even if the new international division of labour still affects
only a restricted number of countries, the transference of jobs
from the West to these newly emerging countries has made committed researchers and activists aware of the changing material
conditions of production. This awareness has in turn demanded a
critical revaluation of traditional economic analysis. The first
change in the conditions of production has occurred in the technological substructure of the global economy. The introduction
of new technology (NT), both in production and in marketing,
has fundamentally altered the nature of business organizations.
The fragmentation of jobs has progressed, especially in manufacturing, to such an extent that the execution of the respective
partial operations of even very sophisticated overall processes
now often requires a training period of not more than a few
weeks, even for a very young and inexperienced worker. One
does not need any formal training in electronics, for example, to
be a worker in the global assembly-line, bonding chips with a
golden wire in the production of integrated circuits or semi-
conductors. In the clothing industry, too, technological changes
have made it possible to automate designing, cutting and finishing – the processes known as skilled in clothing manufacturing.
Only the sewing of garments, known as shell-making in the
trade, remains labour-intensive. This stage of production, like
the assembling of chips in the electronics industry, can be exe-
cuted anywhere; and TNCs with large resources at their disposal,
that make it easy to operate worldwide, have shifted the labour-
intensive aspects of production to cheap labour countries, which
have a vast array of surplus female labour to offer.

The second important change in the material conditions of
production follows from the first, and is manifest in the nature of

the internationalization of capital. It is not that investment by multinationals in non-European countries is a new phenomenon. It existed before, but, prior to the rise of global dispersion of stages of manufacture, the operations of the TNCs duplicated the production process that prevailed in their home countries. Their investments were primarily made to gain access to new markets that would otherwise have been barred to them by import restrictions.

This kind of manufacturing by TNCs, especially in the automobile or pharmaceutical industries, still predominates in those large Latin American countries that were the main sites of investment in the earlier phase of internationalization of capital. The new investments since the 1970s, however, have been linked to a different kind of trade: they involve primarily intra-firm trades of finished and/or intermediate products between two subsidiaries of a transnational corporation.

The definition of a subsidiary firm in the host country is wide: it can cover a broad range of enterprises linked to a TNC by varying degrees of local ownership of equities. The specific characteristic of such commerce nonetheless remains constant. It has to do with the movement of goods in different stages of completion between plants linked to a centrally run corporation. A recent estimate indicates that half of all exports manufactured in developing countries exemplify this type of intra-firm trade.[4] In some newly industrializing countries such as Singapore, the proportion is higher still.

Even these estimates only partially reveal the importance of TNCs in the export-led growth of the middle-income new countries. There are many labour-intensive exporting industries where multinational companies are not directly involved at both ends in production – hence, strictly speaking, they do not represent intra-firm trade. Nonetheless, a large part of even this flow of trade is directly controlled by TNCs, because it is they who finally control the market outlets. Institutional links here take the form of international subcontracting between independent enterprises. This is, for example, a major form of involvement of international capital in the clothing industry. According to the International Textile, Garment and Leather Workers' Federation, foreign procurement through legally independent companies in developing countries is about six times the value of the TNCs' own production in foreign subsidiaries. The Seidensticker group, one of West Germany's large clothing firms, sources nearly 80 per cent of its shirts from cheap labour countries but it owns no shirt factories abroad. Similarly, Tootal, one of the top four British textile multinationals, now procures most of the shirts sold under its labels from abroad, though it has not set up any shirt factories of its own outside the UK.[5] The subcontractors, however, may depend on the TNCs for technical assistance and product designs as well as for threads and fabrics and other materials.

What has been the outcome of this increasing dependence on TNCs of nation-states on an export-led path of development? First and foremost, it has meant the creation of a large number of insecure, and often ill-paid, jobs. The fact that the jobs can be relocated elsewhere gives the TNCs an effective weapon to keep wage costs down both in the home and host countries. The point is well described by a quality control inspector in a US General Electric Company plant in Massachusetts:

> I'll give it to the company: they are great with the public relations bit. GE puts out two, three bulletins a week, and they are always telling the people [the plant's workers] about the foreign competition. What they're trying to do, and they're successful, is getting the idea across that if they don't work harder, if they do not stop taking days off, and quit taking so much time on their coffee-break and so forth, that they are gonna have to take the plant and move it to Singapore . . . By the way, they have a plant in Singapore that makes clocks . . . They have been very successful at the productivity thing, you know. They have scared people with it. This company, like a lot of companies, runs things by fear.[6]

Barnet and Müller, in their book *Global Reach*, have shown with compelling arguments how corporate organization on a world scale has proved to be a highly effective weapon for undercutting the power of organized labour everywhere. Capital, technology and marketplace ideology – all ingredients of corporate power – are mobile; workers, by and large, are less so. As a result, the trade unions have greater difficulty in negotiating with the multinational companies than with the national ones.[7] As a Malaysian trade unionist reported:

> The firms have also let us know that in case of labour trouble or wage demands, they can stop production within a month, and transfer to another neighbouring country with a cheaper labour force in the Asian area.[8]

Even if the labour force remains docile, companies sometimes move when their tax-holidays run out. Japan has apparently developed a barge on which factories can be floated to new sources of cheap labour once a particular lot has been used up.[9] In some cases, the workers are 'used up' in a rather more literal sense. The assembly of silicon chips requires detailed work under a microscope; after three years the eyesight of workers, as Rachael Grossman reports, begins to fail. 'Grandma, where are your glasses?' is a common greeting to electronic workers over 25 years old in Hong Kong.[10] And why 'Grandma'? Because the majority of the workers in the world market factories of the multinationals are women. Employment of women in labour-surplus countries, where male unemployment is staggeringly high, is part of a wider management strategy. The strategy is to derive the maximum benefit from 'the division of labour', by reducing the need for craft skill and thereby the power of organized labour.

It is not a coincidence that the majority of workers in the worldwide factories of the transnational corporations are women. It is not the genetic characteristics of women workers that make them the preferred labour force, but rather their marginal role in the mainstream labour movement. In the new phase of industrial restructuring, therefore, the TNCs' management strategies are geared towards recruiting workers that operate far away from the organized labour on the main factory floor. This goal can be achieved by shifting jobs either to geographically distant locations, as in the Free Trade Zones of South Asia, or to small subcontracting units, such as the family-based sweatshops in Britain's West Midlands or in Italy. The abiding principle is the same: it should be possible to hire and fire workers without much problem.

A job for Jill as Jack goes downhill

The new management strategies, therefore, have brought with them a system of 'flexible manning'; ironically, this has meant an unprecedented rise in the employment of women workers. The expansion in the opportunities for women has been startling in the newly industrializing countries of the Far East (Figure 1), and the same pattern follows in any country that sets out on the well-trodden path of export-led development.

In the Free Trade Zones (FTZs) – the enclaves reserved for the export-led production of the subsidiaries and subcontractors of transnational corporations – nearly 80 per cent of the workers are women. Predictably, they are engaged as direct operatives in assembly-line jobs. The administrative, professional and technical posts, although far fewer in number, are generally taken up by men.[11]

These experiences in the global factories of the TNCs are being chillingly repeated in the so-called First World countries. The employment statistics of OECD countries indicate that between 1960 and 1980 the participation rate of women in the job market has consistently increased (Table 1). The trend has accelerated since then. Explanations for this phenomenon are most commonly sought in supply factors, such as women's increased aspirations, educational inputs, or the need for extra earning in the family.[12] However, the demand factors, which are not stressed sufficiently, have been equally, if not more, important. Employers now actively seek women workers for less secure jobs.

The changing gender structure of employment in the West is indicative of yet another, relatively unexplored dimension of the new international division of labour. In this, the jobs are not re-located to low-wage countries, but are shifted from high-wage secure employment to ill-paid casualized work. As in other advanced countries, the overall level of employment has fallen

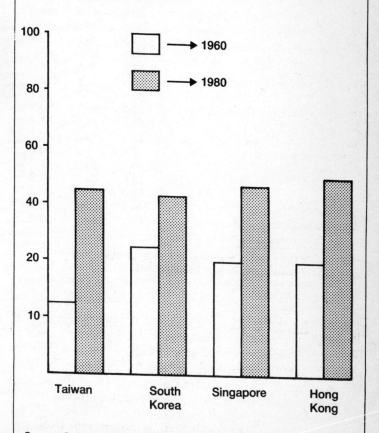

Figure 1: Export-led growth and changing gender-structure of employment

The case of the Asian Gang of Four: percentages of women workers in the official economy

Source: Government Statistics and ILO Yearbooks of Labour Statistics

Table 1: Female labour force of all ages as percentage of female population aged 15-64, in industrialized countries: 1960, 1970, 1980

Country	1960	1970	1980
Australia	33.1	45.1	52.6
Canada	32.0	43.1	57.3
United States	42.6	48.9	59.7
Austria	55.0	49.2	49.2
Belgium	36.2	40.0	48.0
Denmark	43.5	58.0	70.8
Finland	65.9	62.5	67.1
France	46.4	48.2	52.5
Germany, Federal Republic of	49.2	48.1	49.3
Ireland	35.3	34.3	35.2
Italy	37.1	33.5	38.8
Netherlands	26.3	30.3	35.2
Norway	36.3	38.8	63.2
Spain	23.6	28.9	31.9
Sweden	55.0	59.4	74.1
Switzerland	44.8	52.1	49.7
United Kingdom	46.1	50.8	57.6

Sources: OECD: *Labour Force Statistics 1969–80* (Paris 1982);
OECD: *Demographic Trends, 1950–90* (Paris 1979);
ILO: *Yearbook of Labour Statistics* (Geneva), various issues;
national population censuses; national statistics.

dramatically in the UK during the last decade. The growth of jobs on part-time and short-term contracts, by contrast, has been substantial. As Figure 2: A shows, in 1971 only one job in seven was part-time. By 1984, the proportion had become one in five. The majority of the part-timers are women. Dramatic as these figures may be, the rise in this type of job shows only one facet of the total phenomenon of casualization. As the survey by the In-stitute of Manpower Studies at Sussex University revealed, nearly 7.6 per cent of the workers in the UK in 1985 were in tem-porary employment. The projection into the future also shows an upward trend. Significantly two-thirds of such temporary em-

---

Women receive casual employment in all sectors: Japan as an example

At Honda Motor Co.'s Wako factory, part-time women workers are hired at its engine assembly line. In all, 48 part-time women workers serve engine assembly work, assisted by material handling robots. At its engine inspection stations part-time women workers check assembled engines with the aid of automatic inspection devices. In its administration office computers, facsimile equipment, word processors and other office automation systems have been introduced and the company is preparing for hiring part-time women clerical workers on office work after graduating from its short-period training courses. Certainly, the progress of the mechatronics facilitates employment of part-time women workers, as seen at Honda factory.

After the 1973 oil crisis, women workers hired by business at part-time basis increased rapidly. According to the government statistics, about 1.7 million women workers were hired at part-time in 1973. In 1982 they amounted to 2.48 million. During the nine-year period, the number of women part-time jobbers increased by 67%. By definition, part-time workers are those who work less than 35 hours a week. But, in reality, there are many part-time women workers who work as hard as permanent women workers.

Source: Committee for the Protection of Women in the Computer World, Tokyo, 1983.

Temp. work

ployment is given to women.[13] The less secure jobs, generally, have gone to women. The resultant shift in the gender structure of employment in the UK (Figure 2: B) mirrors the experience of all Western countries and Japan and points to a new thrust in the restructuring of capital. This restructuring, as with the spatial division of labour, is fundamentally based on the accepted division of work in the domestic sphere. As it is the women who are deemed responsible for housework and childcare, it is considered normal for them to be satisfied with ill-paid and insecure jobs.

The advantages to the employers are clear. To quote *Lloyds Bank Economic Bulletin* of November 1985:

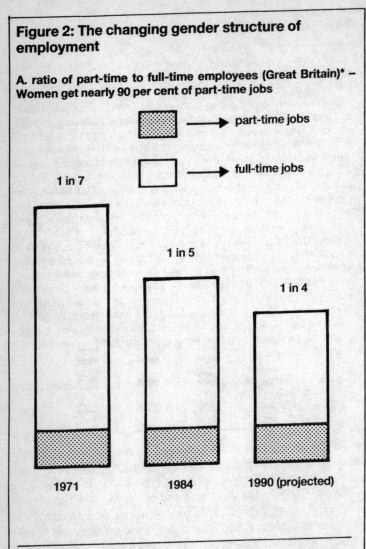

Figure 2: The changing gender structure of employment

A. ratio of part-time to full-time employees (Great Britain)* –
Women get nearly 90 per cent of part-time jobs

part-time jobs

full-time jobs

1 in 7

1 in 5

1 in 4

1971   1984   1990 (projected)

Source: Employment Gazette and Lloyds Bank Economic Bulletin, November 1985

* (nearest approximation to round numbers)

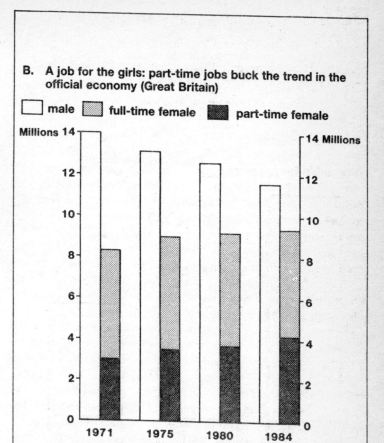

B. A job for the girls: part-time jobs buck the trend in the official economy (Great Britain)

□ male   ▨ full-time female   ■ part-time female

Source: *Employment Gazette* and *Lloyds Bank Economic Bulletin*, November 1985

More and more employers are now overcoming their initial resistance to part-time jobs on grounds of higher personnel management costs. Part-timers can be used to meet peaks of work activity, or to operate expensive machinery on shifts around the clock; their pay per hour is lower to the employer . . . and their productivity is probably higher per hour than that of full-time workers.

The recruitment of part-time workers is therefore an effective way of intensifying the work process. Also, this form of employment frees the employer from the threat of unionization.

The growth of part-time work in the affluent West is commonly associated with the expansion of jobs in the services sector, where women are traditionally clustered as workers in the lower grades, and of jobs such as those of cleaners, shop-assistants, secretaries and clerks. There has been very little promotion of women to the upper rungs of the ladder in the services sector, although women predominate numerically in this sector as a whole. In the last few years, however, women workers have also been making numerical gains in the manufacturing sector. This change is becoming particularly visible now that international capital is returning from Third World countries to the peripheral regions of the advanced West. The example of Merseyside or Lower Clydeside in the UK is typical. Here, as the traditional industries like steel, coal and shipbuilding die, the number of men joining the dole queues increases. In place of the traditional industries, transnational electronic companies move in to make use of labour whose bargaining power has been substantially weakened. But these companies, as in the new towns of Scotland, significantly employ only women on the assembly line. It is not surprising, therefore, that the proportion of jobs in some areas of Wales and Scotland is perceptibly changing in favour of women. Most of the managerial and technical jobs, however, there as elsewhere, are still held by men.[14]

Women workers in the submerged economy

The management strategy of the global corporations, in other words, is to rely on a docile, non-unionized and casual work-force. If such labour is available near the market, it makes little sense to source production in offshore countries. There are definite advantages in having the sources of supply nearer the market: the companies are less encumbered by tariff barriers, and can respond quickly to changes in demand.

With rising unemployment in the West, it is not difficult now to find cheap female labour near the market. It is not surprising that even in the traditionally 'runaway' industries such as clothing and toy manufacturing, increased subcontracting domestically is now reducing the need for international subcontracting. In many other unlikely areas, the advent of microelectronic technology is speeding up the system of domestic putting-out. A dramatic miniaturization of machines and tools means that even products whose manufacture requires heavy engineering may not need a huge floor-space. Information technology also allows management to co-ordinate scattered units of production effectively. What NT has meant, therefore, is that most large factories can now be viewed as collections of various small production processes that can readily be dispersed. The only concern that management would have is that the costs of co-ordination and of transporting intermediate products should be outweighed by the savings in labour costs achieved through decentralization. The biggest savings in smaller units are, of course, bound up with the ease with which employment and labour legislation can thus be avoided.

The logical extension of the system of subcontracting (called 'flexible specialization' in the US) is the rise of homeworking, both in high- and low-tech industries in Western economies. Terms such as networking, new technology homeworking, and distance homeworking all refer to new types of self-employment, in which workers are dependent on big companies for orders but are not entitled to the benefits enjoyed by employees in an office. Again, women are the preferred labour force in this area, as it is considered desirable for them to be able to work from home; in this way, they are not distracted from their 'true profession' of being homemakers.

New technology homeworking, although a growing phenomenon, is still less significant in numerical terms than traditional manufacturing homework. This type of putting-out has made such a comeback in the Western world that it almost harks back to the Victorian era. The workers in the sweatshop economy and in home-based units are invariably the most vulnerable in society. They are, as I indicated, predominantly black and women workers. Their jobs are rarely registered in the official employment statistics. They form part of a growing hidden economy in the affluent West. Despite their invisibility in the official statistics, their presence is unmistakably reflected in the origins of the merchandise sold by high-street retailers.[15] In the early 1980s a bewildered child was reported to have asked whether Father Christmas lived in Hong Kong. Her question would surely be different now. Father Christmas increasingly buys products made in Europe. Curiously, however, there is no concomitant increase in official employment figures to account for his marked change of preference.

Casualization of work and the new proletariat

If we were to include the workers in the hidden economy, the proportion of women in the total workforce would show an even bigger rise than that reflected in official statistics. In short, women are getting more jobs because, with the advent of NT, most jobs are becoming ill-paid, insecure or part-time.

Till now, the impact of NT has been more pronounced in the casualization of work than in bringing automation. The reasons for this depend on cool economic factors. The major advances in technology have allowed employers to conceptualize the individual elements in production and to think them out in terms of the logic of machinery. In fact, until the elements are separated this way, it is impossible to contemplate their complete mechanization. Once an element is thus separated, its execution may no longer require the craft-skill that has a property of creative mystery. But the fragmentation of a job into its elementary operations does not necessarily lead to automation. The decision to automate depends on the relative costs of machines and the wages of the available unskilled labour. With the vast improvements in transport, communication and information technology, TNCs can now have access to a worldwide reserve army of labour, consisting overwhelmingly of black women in non-European countries, and of women, again in many cases black women, in the West. While they provide cheap and non-unionized labour, it makes little sense to invest in expensive machines.

The implications of the managerial control that advances in technology can confer were fully explored by Charles Babbage as early as 1835.[16] The subdivision of the production process into simple elements offers capitalists an effective means to cheapen the manufacturing costs of commodities by maximum replacement of craft-skill labour. They can then buy labour power which needs only the minimum craft-skill for each respective element, and which therefore can 'always be purchased at an easy rate'. In other words, it is a means of counteracting the 'excessive' demands, and what Andrew Ure (1835) and Frederick Taylor (1903) described as the 'moodiness', of skilled workers.[17] Provided there are no effective workers' organizations, workers are then forced to compete against one another on the overcrowded labour market for unskilled and semi-skilled jobs. This competition keeps the level of wages down. It is indeed the most powerful reason behind the constant attempts by capitalists to fragment complex labour processes into a large number of uncomplex operations.

Babbage's principle of the accumulation of capital was analysed by Marx, and has been discussed in recent times, as by Harry Braverman in 1974, as the general law of the capitalist division of labour.[18] The focus has been on the economic and social consequences of this principle in individual developed capitalist societies. The state of technology today, however, makes it possible, especially for the transnational corporations, to embark on an international division of labour such as Babbage could not have foreseen.

As Fröbel, Heinrichs and Kreye have shown in their brilliant work entitled *The New International Division of Labour* (1980), the increased surplus of international capital depends precisely on the worldwide allocation of separate elements of production to the labour that is cheapest or best adapted.[19] What they do not emphasize sufficiently, however, is the sexual and racial basis of this emergent division of labour. The changing gender structure of employment, both in European and non-European countries, reveals that the TNCs now deliberately recruit female workers, in whom they see the promise of 'subservience, obedience and punctuality', the moral qualities so glorified by Babbage, Ure and Taylor. In their search for this ideal labour force, the global corporations have thus created a new female proletariat in specific locations in virtually all regions of the world. In the process, ironically enough, they have become instrumental in creating the basis for a new sense of solidarity among women workers, leading them to the organizing of a novel labour movement.

Mitter emphasises sexual + racial basis of the emergent division of labour which writers such as fröbel, Heinrichs and Kreye (1980) do not sufficiently elaborate on.

+ emphasises international level

2. Runaway capital

The flight of capital

The export-oriented industrialization (EOI) of the newly emerging countries was necessarily linked to the changed management strategies of the global corporations. Since the exports of these countries began to consist mainly of semi-finished products, completed only in their labour-intensive stages and sent abroad by the subcontractors or subsidiaries of the global corporations, the growth through EOI hardly improved the bargaining power of the host states. But what it successfully achieved was containment of wage bargaining power of white male workers in the First World through the use of women workers in the Third.

This move was essential for restoring the profit of global corporations in a recession-ridden world economy. The promise of a docile young female workforce at the periphery stood in sharp contrast to the assertive and high-cost male workforce in the organized sectors of the First World. By the 1970s, organized labour in the United States had truly become a fetter on profit-making there. The real rate of return on all manufacturing investments of 15.5 per cent in the years 1963–6, fell to 12.7 per cent in 1967–70. It then fell to 10.1 per cent in 1971-4, reaching an average of 9.7 per cent for the period 1974–8.[1] In contrast, the profits earned in Third World countries could be staggeringly high. 'I should not really tell you this,' a vice-president of a US-based global bank confided to Barnet and Müller, 'but while we earn around 13 to 14 per cent on our US operations, we can easily count on a 33 per cent rate of return on the business conducted in Latin America.' An assistant to the president of a large US-based global corporation told the same authors that it was 'no problem' to maintain real rates of return from 50 to 400 per cent in some Third World countries.[2]

What the peripheral countries had in large measure that the US did not, was a vast pool of reserve labour. In fact, capital's ability to restore profit by using the labour reserve at home had been declining since the Second World War, because of full employment in the West. While there existed a plentiful and vulnerable supply of illegal immigrant labour from Latin America, the cheap labour status of both women and blacks had been relatively undermined since the late 1960s. In the United States, as everywhere else, women's position in the job market had depended considerably on an ideology that defined women primarily as wives and mothers. Their presence in the labour force was viewed as temporary, and their role merely as that of the secondary breadwinner in the family. The massive and permanent incorporation of women into the labour force during the postwar period to a large extent changed the stereotyped image of women workers. Also, the underlying social changes, such as an increase in the number of single-parent families headed by women, led to a growing contradiction between ideology and reality that exploded in the women's movement. The major demand of the movement was equal employment opportunities for women as well as equal pay for equal work. To what extent it managed to achieve this goal in the States remains an open question. But the movement itself signalled the fact that a renewed capitalist expansion based on women's cheaper labour status was, at best, problematic.[3]

Blacks did not provide a good alternative either. The coming of age of the second generation of Southern black migrants and their numerical ascendancy in the labour force led to new racial and social conflict in the North. The black militant movement gave a voice to the frustrated expectations of a new generation of black workers. Although illegal immigrants from the Caribbean and Latin America provided an alternative labour reserve, the other way to restore profit was to take some of the labour-intensive part of the work to cheap labour countries. The legislative framework defining import control policy was made favourable to the move as well. From the mid-1960s onwards, tariff laws in the States were amended, thus giving a boost to the TNCs' overseas investments. Items 806.30 and 807.00 in the US Tariff

Schedules permitted goods to be shipped abroad for processing with a duty that was to be paid *only* on the value added. Between 1966 and 1972, exports from less developed countries to the United States increased at a rate of 12 per cent annually, but exports of semi-finished products, originally shipped from the US, increased at a rate of 60 per cent.[4]

Flights of capital have taken a similar trend in Western Europe, especially since the early 1970s, for comparable reasons. Until the mid-1960s, the bargaining power of labour was successfully contained for two reasons. First, there was the successful mobilization of a large reserve of peasant workers that still existed in Western Europe. But the second and more important reason lay in the massive immigration of black or 'coloured' workers from ex-colonies, as well as from other peripheral countries such as Turkey, Cyprus or Yugoslavia. In fact, by restraining wage increases, immigration became a vital precondition of growth and capital accumulation in Western Europe.[5] Black workers, both as guest workers and as colonial migrants, played a key role in the renewal of Western Europe. Invariably, they were segregated in jobs which white workers did not want. As one company manager explained:

> We began employing coloured workers in 1956. You could not get good white workers unless you were prepared to pay over the odds, and good coloured people are better than bad white people. You cannot get good white people to do the menial tasks that have to be done in any foundry, not even floating workers like the Irish.[6]

Migrant workers took the unwanted jobs in Europe – the lowest paid and the lowest skilled – and were used effectively to arrest the decline of corporate profit. The combined total of 16 million people of non-European origin contributed substantially to the post-war reconstruction of Europe. Their readiness to undertake night shift work saved the British textile industry, for example, at the time. In France, a highly organized network was set up to recruit workers in Africa and put them to work on French building-sites, where they also had to live. Sprawling shanty-towns of tin huts, housing African workers, sprang up around all major

French cities where construction projects were under way. The car industries of France and Germany depended heavily on migrant workers, as did some of the electrical giants like Bosch and Siemens.

But in spite of the commercial advantages, the arrival of large numbers of black immigrants, especially in the inner-city areas of a metropolis, created social and political tensions. With the onset of recession and rising unemployment, they easily became scapegoats: a racist backlash soon became widespread in Europe, and fed the growth of racist groups such as the Front National in France (which in 1985 gained over 10 per cent of the vote in the Euro-elections). West Germany put a ban on the recruitment of non-EEC workers in 1973, and Britain, France and the Netherlands changed immigration and nationality laws to stop the entry of non-European workers from their former colonies.[7]

The changed situation made it difficult for the TNCs to continue using the reserve army of labour that had been theirs through immigration. The existing pool of black workers also

---

European hospitality

Sociologists have found a very convenient explanation, one that has been adopted by everybody, including left-wing parties such as the French Socialist and Communist parties. It is a matter of the famous 'threshold of tolerance': with more than a certain percentage (10 or 11 per cent) of foreigners in a particular living-space, the risks of intolerance of the Other are real and can lead to dramatic incidents. So, in order to avoid reactions of racist violence, the space must be appropriately rationed. At this point an unexpected perversity creeps in: it would seem that some foreigners are less foreign than others. Thus immigrants belonging to the sphere of Judaeo-Christian civilization, like the Portuguese, Spaniards and Italians, would appear to be better tolerated today than those who come from too different a culture, such as the Moslem one (Arabs and Turks). Perhaps the European immigrants adapt better than the others. They also feel themselves better accepted.

Source: Tahar Ben Jelloun, *Hospitalité française*, Paris: Seuil 1984, p. 87.

increasingly became politicized and assertive. To quote A. Sivanandan:

> . . . blacks by 1968 were beginning to fight as a class and as a people. Whatever the specifics of resistance in the respective communities and however difficult the strategies and lines of struggle, the experience of a common racism and a common fight against the state united them at the barricades.[8]

The resultant attitudes were not compatible with management strategies that looked for acquiescent labour in black migrant workers. So-called 'second generation' immigrants – Europeans by birth but excluded from European identity by the colour of their skin – were even more unlikely to provide the preferred labour force, as their frustration, arising from economic and social discrimination, moved them from 'the state of resistance to rebellion'.[9]

Offshore assembly work by Japanese multinationals was also necessitated by the specific state of capital accumulation in Japan, which had gravely depleted the labour reserve at home by the 1970s. Until then the major source of additional workers required by the continuous and rapid accumulation of capital in Japan had been the agricultural sector. As the size of the agricultural and forestry sector in the total labour force declined from 49 per cent in 1950 to 16 per cent in 1970, the labour market began to tighten. Makoto Itoh describes the situation:

> . . . by 1973, the number of job vacancies surpassed the number of job seekers by 83% and average nominal wages in the private sector went up . . . between 1965 and 1973 real wages in manufacturing industry more than doubled and between 1970 and 1973 they exceeded the growth in productivity . . . the increase in real wages and prices of raw materials (especially of oil) pulled down the rate of profit of Japanese industrial and commercial firms from 22.7% in 1970 to 14.7% in 1973.[10]

One possible way of restoring profit, therefore, was to transfer a range of labour-intensive assembling jobs to cheap-labour countries.

The rationale behind such relocations of production by American, European or Japanese firms was straightforward. The manager of a foreign-owned firm in Malaysia summarily explained how profitable these moves could be: one worker working for an hour in Malaysia produces enough to pay the wages of ten workers working one shift, plus all the costs of materials and transport (Table 2). The workers, significantly, are all women: black and coloured women, with their 'natural patience' and 'manual dexterity', are expected to make perfect employees. As an American consultant who solicits US business for the Bermuda Industrial Park in Ciudad Juarez on the Mexican-American border says: 'You don't have any sullenness here. They all smile.'[11]

Table 2: Cheap labour in the Third World: average hourly earnings in electronics and garment-manufacturing (Figures are in US dollars)

Country			Electronics	Garments
Hong Kong	1980	(1)	0.97	1.03
Korea	1980	(1)	0.91	0.59
Malaysia	1980	(2)	0.42	–
Philippines	1978	(2)	0.30	0.17
Singapore	1980	(1)	0.90	0.80
Sri Lanka	1981	(2)	–	0.12
Japan	1980	(1)	5.97	3.56
USA	1980	(1)	6.96	4.57

Sources: (1) ILO Yearbook of Labour Statistics, 1981
(2) ARTEP Case Studies

Quoted from G. Edgren, 'Spearheads of Industrialisation or Sweatshops in the Sun?' ILO-ARTEP, 1982.

Women in the peripheral states

It would be unfair, however, to ascribe the industrialization of the Third World countries *only* to the internationalization process of capital. The politics of class and gender in Third World countries likewise play important roles in the launching of export-oriented development plans.

In the 1950s and 1960s, political independence removed many restrictions which colonial rule had imposed on the production of industrial goods in the peripheral and semi-peripheral countries especially in South and South-east Asia. Soon a strong ruling group emerged in these countries, keenly committed to a policy of state support for national industrialization. Hence the entry of TNCs into semi-peripheral countries had to involve careful linking of international capital to the goals of national reconstruction. Only in this way could international capital gain access to cheap labour, as well as larger internal markets, in the developing economies.

The emerging newly independent countries initially, in the l950s, decided on a policy of import-substitution (IS). This confronted TNCs with particularly thorny problems. The policy involved, through a combination of investment incentives and import tariffs, the establishment of industries producing for the domestic market the goods that were previously imported. Initially the policy enjoyed considerable success, leading to a more diversified industrial structure. In Malaysia the paper and printing industry, the beverage, food and tobacco, textile and electrical appliance industries, all grew behind the tariff protection. In the Philippines the IS policy laid the foundation for light consumer goods industries such as processed foods, shoes and garments, where domestic products could compete successfully with the more expensive imported items. But in spite of its early success, the policy was doomed to failure in most countries because of the nature of investments.

The thrust of the import-substitution policy tended to provide luxury items for the urban-based elites at the expense of necessary investment in the infrastructure of the rural areas, where the majority of the people lived in abject poverty. The consequence of this was that the policy generally foundered because of the narrowness of the domestic market for high-cost locally manufactured luxury goods. Moreover, the IS policy was often very inefficient, as it relied on highly protected markets and on expensive imported inputs. The crisis of foreign exchange became permanent, as it was politically more difficult to close down a factory than it was to restrict 'inessential' imports. Hence, the country was often left with a disproportionate bill for essential imports of raw materials and parts to make the 'inessential' goods whose import was previously restricted.

In this situation, export-oriented industrialization (EOI), with the investment of transnational corporations, opened up a new way of fulfilling the aspirations of the elite groups in developing countries. Establishing 'export-platforms', as nuclei of future industrialization, offered a ready market abroad and relieved the crucial blockage of foreign exchange. By circumventing the problems that followed from IS, the new policy strengthened the power-base of the ruling elites, who forged an alliance with the transnational corporations. Teresa Hayter sums up the class composition of this new alliance:

> Alliances shift. Traditionally, there has been an alliance between landowners, who are interested in agricultural exports and in cheap imports of luxury goods, and foreign private investors; local manufacturers have sometimes been hostile to foreigners, who threaten them with take-overs and bankruptcy, but they are also often prepared to throw in their lot with the multinationals, who offer them comfortable salaries and a certain show of prestige; government officials can be bribed and won over, directly by foreign companies and less directly by official aid agencies on the look-out for 'our man'; and governments themselves usually know very well which side their bread is buttered, for it is certain that the West can come to their support in subversive times with offers of military and financial aid, temporary rescue from their debt problems, and an assurance that at least some imports will continue to flow.[12]

The inspiration for the new model was given to the ruling elites of the Third World by Brazil and South Korea. The focal point of the 'Brazilian Miracle' was an almost sevenfold increase in exports of manufactured goods to advanced industrialized countries between 1968 and 1973. At the centre of the export drive were labour-intensive commodities such as shoes, Brazil's most spectacular export, which went up from $2 million to $200 million in only seven years.

The 'South Korea Miracle' was equally impressive. As one World Bank consultant glowingly described it,

> with real GNP rising about 10 per cent a year in the one-and-a-half decades following the policy reform of the early sixties, [South] Korea was one of the star performers of the world economy. Rapid economic growth was achieved under an export-oriented strategy that led to increases in the value of exports of goods and services at approximately 27 per cent a year.[13]

With their obsessive fixation on growth rates, World Bank planners tended to play down the conditions that were bound up with the 'successes' in South Korea and Brazil: the systematic depression of wages, and the existence of a military state. As Walden Bello and his collaborators have shown, the most significant consequence of the class-bias in this particular mode of development became evident in the national accounts figures. In Brazil, for example, the income of the lowest paid 40 per cent of the population remained practically stagnant between 1960 and 1970, while that of the top 5 per cent increased by over 80 per cent. As a result, the share in the national income of 95 per cent of the population declined from 73 per cent to 64 per cent. The rich became richer, and the theory that wealth would 'trickle down' remained just a dream.

A turn from import-substitution to an export-oriented policy did not improve the level of investment in the rural sector. If anything, depressing the economic situation of rural areas became a precondition of the new approach. The new international division of labour, based on EOI, was supposed to encourage development in a 'natural' way, merely using the 'comparative advantages' that a given country enjoys and without the tampering that goes with rigorous planning. But in effect the countries embracing the new approach demanded that the economy be structured in a particular way. In order to entice transnational investment, these countries had to improve the 'comparative advantage' of cheap labour a) by keeping down the real wages in the urban sector by ensuring a control on the prices of primary products; and b) by increasing the supply of the 'reserve army of labour' through impoverishment of the rural sector. To quote an International Labour Organization (ILO) monograph:

> The Thai Government thus not only devoted a lot of aid funds into developing communications and other parts of the country's infrastructure, but also tried to keep primary prices down. This was not done to a great extent by obvious strong-arm methods, such as price controls. Mostly, it involved policies designed not to channel too much social investment into the countryside, not doing anything which would raise the expectations or the bargaining power of the farmers, not allowing the rural interests to develop any real political torque.[14]

Deteriorating terms of trade in the primary sector led to a massive exodus of labour from agriculture in Thailand and other Third World countries. The depressed rural sector thereby provided a ready supply of recruits into the urban labour force, and this kept down the price of labour. The supply of cheap food also helped to counteract greater wage demands by urban workers. The resultant economic advantages of the labour proved specially attractive to TNCs. The quality of Thai labour, for example, was widely advertised:

> While the minimum daily rate in Bangkok is supposed to be 54 baht (US $2.70), it will be only 47 baht (US $2.35) in the Central and Southern regions and a mere 44 baht (US $2.20) in the North and North-east . . . Thai workers have been found by many companies to be willing, dextrous, remarkably quick learners and conscientious, dependable workers . . . Another point about Thai labour is that it is not militant. There have been many strikes, of course, but in general most disputes are settled amicably and indeed, this year [1980], some of the country's labour leaders have said publicly that they will accept whatever wage increases

the government deems suitable. The reason for this stand is that labour leaders understand the present situation in the country and have decided that unity is more important than large wage increases.[15]

In some other Third World countries, an exodus of rural labour was triggered not by an absolute lack of investment in the agricultural sector but by a policy that encouraged a rapid expansion of commercial export agriculture at the expense of food crops and the subsistence sector. In the Philippines, for example, cultivated land devoted to rice declined from 3.2 million hectares in 1960 to 3.1 million hectares in 1970. In the early 1970s, export agriculture continued its relentless advance, with the blessings of the World Bank. The amount of land devoted to sugar, coconuts, pineapples, bananas and other commercial crops increased by 650,000 hectares between 1970 and 1976, and by the end of the 1970s over 30 per cent of the country's 10 million hectares of cultivated land was planted with export crops.

This expansion of export agriculture was not a purely spontaneous process sparked by an international demand for tropical commodities. It was, in fact, part and parcel of the strategy of 'export-led growth' promoted by the Marcos regime and the World Bank. By the mid-1970s, the pineapple plantations of Del Monte and Castles and Cooke on the island of Mindanao had grown to 35,000 hectares and employed some 20,000 workers. Even more remarkable was the expansion in commercial banana production. Impelled by a rising demand for tropical fruits in Japan and the discovery that the soil of south-eastern Mindanao was perfect for growing bananas, the industry spread rapidly and became almost overnight one of the country's top foreign exchange earners. By 1978, banana exports came to $84 million, 15,000 hectares were planted in bananas and 20,000 workers and contract growers were dependent on the industry.

The major cost of the expansion of export agriculture was borne by the thousands of smallholders dispossessed of their land either by outright land-grabs, or land-title frauds, or by their forced or voluntary entry into strictly regimented contract growing arrangements with the agri-business giants. Also, as hundreds of thousands of hectares of cultivated land were turned over to sugar, coconut, pineapple and banana growing, export crop expansion contributed to the increasing inability of the country to be self-sufficient in staple foods. Between 1960 and 1972 – twelve years of rapid export-crop expansion – rice imports rose from $2 million to $34 million.[16]

This was the period when the World Bank and other aid-giving agencies offered the glittering promise of the 'Green Revolution' to Third World countries: a revolution that with its 'miracle seed' and chemical fertilizers was to dispel the hunger of millions of people. This solution seemed particularly attractive where there was a crisis in export-led agriculture. For many peasants, however, the promise was offset by the soaring costs of the fertilizers and imported chemical inputs necessary for higher yields, and by the low resistance of the 'miracle seeds' to tropical diseases and weather conditions. The benefits of the capital-intensive agri-technology accrued mainly to landowners and not to the tillers of the soil or the smallholders. The Green Revolution in fact managed to strengthen the power structure in favour of the rural elites. Trapped by an oppressive land-tenure system, poor tenants were squeezed out of their landholdings.

Displaced and proletarianized by export agriculture and the Green Revolution, the Third World peasantry swelled the labour reserve of the urban areas. There, the society offered three different ways of linking their lives to the global economic system: a) by encouraging them to emigrate to First World countries to sell their labour; b) by offering them jobs in the export-processing industries owned by the multinationals; and c) by pushing them into prostitution for the Japanese, European and American tourists, with the direct connivance of the government. The use of labour power in all these occupations contributed substantially to the foreign exchange-earning mechanisms of the state; and in all three kinds of occupation, women workers were expected to play a far more important role than men. This is bound up with some widespread and deeply rooted preconceptions about characteristically 'feminine' attributes that seemingly make docile and dexterous women suitable for jobs that are repetitive, monotonous or degrading. The domestic skills and the resultant dexterity, for instance, which girls learn from their mothers from early childhood are not intrinsically feminine, but, as Diane Elson and Ruth Pearson have observed,[17] are socially invisible and privatized, and hence do not count as skills for rewarding jobs in a patriarchally dominated public world. In other words, women make cheap workers.

Export of female labour

For some Third World countries, remittances sent home by nationals working abroad have now become a major source of foreign exchange. The Philippines, Bangladesh and Sri Lanka are examples of such countries. In the Philippines, the export of human labour has become an integral part of the export-oriented development programme. By 1979, the Philippine government was earning $1 billion a year from foreign remittances, nearly 15 per cent of its total export earnings. Recruitment and the sending of remittances were not left to the personal choice of the workers either. The Philippines Overseas Employment Administration Agency was instructed by the government to conduct a census of unemployed skilled industrial workers and to advertise a 'skilled package' for jobs overseas. In 1983, to increase the amount of currency coming back to the Philippines, the government passed a decree which compelled a large number of Filipino workers abroad to remit between 50 and 80 per cent of their wages. The penalty for non-compliance would be refusal to renew or extend passports, non-renewal of employment contracts, and, in cases of subsequent violations, repatriation to the Philippines.[18]

The drive to export labour accelerated with an increase in the export-oriented development planning in the Philippines. The *Far Eastern Economic Review* of 26 September 1980 states:

> In only five years the Philippines has graduated into the first division of labour-exporting nations, with a present ranking, according to the Ministry of Labour and Employment (MOLE), of No. 7 worldwide. The marketing of talent, muscle and training brought foreign exchange remittances . . . that compared impressively with mer-

chandise export receipts of $1.74 billion. The number of men and women placed abroad in 1979 represents a four-fold increase over the previous five years.

The exact number of Filipino migrant workers in any country is not known. Many of them enter a country as tourists and stay on to work. In Britain, there are an estimated 20,000 Filipino migrants working as domestics, hotel and hospital workers. In West Germany also there are an estimated 20,000 working as nurses or midwives. In Spain there are 6,000, and in Italy over 15,000, mostly employed as domestic workers. Significantly, most of the Filipino migrants who come to Europe are women, a large percentage of whom are trained as professionals: nurses, teachers, midwives, social workers. In the host country, they are often forced to accept low incomes and to work long, hard hours. In the process, they nonetheless earn substantial foreign currency, which is needed for the development of their country.

The contribution of women, however, is most crucial in providing a workforce in the Export Processing Zones of their home countries – the zones that have been aptly described as 'sweatshops in the sun'.[19]

Sweatshops in the sun

The culmination of the alliance of interests between the multi-nationals and the ruling elite in Third World countries was the establishment of Free Trade Zones or Export Processing Zones. These are focal points of the export-led industrialization policy of the peripheral nations. The term 'Free Trade Zone' itself is semantically curious: it implies almost total freedom for the investing companies from the fiscal as well as the labour legislation of the host country, and an almost complete lack of freedom for the workers, who become deprived of employment rights and the right of unionization.

The principle of the Export Processing Zone (EPZ) is basically that of the freeport. It is a designated area within a country where certain types of goods, often raw materials or components, can be imported, processed into finished goods and re-exported

The Free Trade Zone carrot for foreign companies

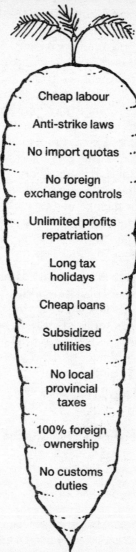

Cheap labour

Anti-strike laws

No import quotas

No foreign
exchange controls

Unlimited profits
repatriation

Long tax
holidays

Cheap loans

Subsidized
utilities

No local
provincial
taxes

100% foreign
ownership

No customs
duties

Source: Women Working Worldwide (see bibliography)

without payment of the usual import and export duties. Modern governments have added a variety of other incentives to the simple privilege of exemption from duties. They are the provision of an infrastructure, tax-exemption, free repatriation of profits and freedom from foreign exchange controls, provisions of loans at favourable rates of interest and in most cases official discouragement of trade unions. The last characteristic is accompanied by the freedom of the investing companies to hire and to fire workers without having to pay much attention to laws concerning workers' rights and health and safety regulations.

To the World Bank, an Export Processing Zone is purely functional, 'a specialized industrial estate located physically and/or administratively outside the customs barrier, oriented to export production. Its facilities serve as a showcase to attract investors and a convenience for their getting established, and are usually associated with other incentives'.[20] But in practice it is more than a showcase: it is a new form of colonialism – with the connivance of the local ruling elites. To quote Takeo:

> Free Trade Zones are like a country within a country. Cut off by barbed wire or concrete walls from the rest of the country and guarded in some cases by 'zone police', the zone is an enclave in terms of customs-territorial aspects and possibly other aspects such as total or partial exemption from laws and decrees of the country concerned . . . The zone has its own authority to which the central government functions are largely delegated . . . workers employed in the zone are often subject to special regulations (prohibition of labour disputes, for instance), have to show special passes to enter it and must often undergo a body check when they finish a day's toil . . . As a right-wing Japanese businessman, Yukawa Kohei put it 'the free trade zone is a new form of foreign settlement adapted to the new situation.'[21]

The first freeport was established in Shannon in Ireland in the late 1950s, but the idea soon spread to developing Third World countries as a new way to entice foreign investment. There are now 52 zones in operation in developing countries, primarily devoted to manufacturing for export. Twenty of these were set up in Asia and 20 in the Caribbean and Latin America. The first African zone was set up in Mauritius in the mid-1970s, and this is the most successful of all African EPZs, employing nearly 17,500 workers, mainly in the assembling of textiles and garments. In the developing world, more than one million workers are now employed in the EPZ areas, and on average 80 per cent of them are women. Of this female proletariat of nearly a million, almost 70 per cent are in South and South-east Asia. Even communist China has started to set up such zones along its borders in Hong Kong, in order to be linked to the global economy through the fullest utilization of its comparative advantage: cheap female labour.

Maquiladoras

The spread of EPZs has also taken a new form over the years: in some places, it has become an institutional concept rather than a territorial one. In the case of Sri Lanka, for example, the EPZ system has tended to spread over the whole country. In India too, the system governing firms operating in the Kandla EPZ is tending to spread to all firms, whatever their location, whose production is destined exclusively for export markets. The facilities granted to these firms, especially as regards importing more easily from abroad, are tending significantly to reduce the specific attraction of the geographical areas of the EPZs themselves.[22] The domestic resources, as a result, are being increasingly mobilized for the world market.

The spread of the institution all over a country is significant in those places where, as in India, the magnitude of the unemployment problem is such that a geographically confined EPZ could make very little contribution. The 'maquiladora' system of Mexico has become the model of export-oriented growth for these countries. This system, as defined by the Mexican legislators in 1965, refers to subcontracting companies, specially designed for foreign industrialists, which enjoy freedom from customs duties. At first, such companies could be set up only in the frontier zone, at the border between Mexico and the United States, as part of the Border Industrialization Programme, but this restriction was modified in 1970 and 1972. There was thus a switch from a 'closed system' to an 'open system', the firm being entirely free to set up anywhere in the country. The concept of the EPZ thus became one of status rather than of geographical location.

The institution of maquiladoras in fact covers two situations: that of established firms which supply the domestic market and whose excess production capacity can be oriented towards export activities, and that of foreign enterprises coming to set up. In both cases, the intention is to reduce unemployment, which is particularly rife in the frontier area of northern Mexico, where the demographic growth rate is very high and the population doubles every 10 years. In fact it was in order to avoid overconcentration of workers in the north that the maquiladora was freed from the obligation to be located only in the border area.

By 1980 the maquiladora system had led to the creation of 120,000 jobs in Mexico; most of the jobs are in electronics and clothing, and almost all the workers are women. This is significant, as the Border Industrialization Programme was originally introduced to combat the rising unemployment among Mexican males in the area, which had resulted from the United States' sudden and unilateral termination in 1964 of the Mexican labour programme. This, commonly known as the Bracero programme, had for two decades regulated the transfer of agricultural labourers from Mexico to the south-west of the United States. With the termination of the programme by the US government, the economic problems along the border were accentuated. Two hundred thousand 'braceros' (literally 'labourers') were abruptly faced with unemployment; at the same time, a growing number of agricultural workers continued to migrate to the border from the interior of Mexico and from Guatemala. Unemployment rates reached 50 per cent in some places where displaced 'braceros' settled in border communities. Political unrest became a real possibility.

The Border Industrialization Programme (BIP) in 1965

offered a logical solution to this problem. It appeared attractive
since it was so 'simple in approach'. BIP was seen as a mechanism

> to merge American capital and technical knowledge with
> relatively inexpensive Mexican labour. As such, attempts
> are made to lure American enterprise to the region by con-
> tending that labour costs are significantly lower. The pro-
> gram is analagous in many ways to other ongoing US oper-
> ations in Korea . . . and Hong Kong.[23]

The maquiladora system, although it came to be extended ter-
ritorially, has remained most successful in the border area of
Mexico. BIP provided an ideal situation for US businessmen
wishing to operate in Mexico but reluctant to forego the
'American way of life'. Maquiladoras in the interior of Mexico
cannot offer such privileges:

> The advantages to the US manager, his family and his com-
> pany, are substantial. The company avoids the expense of
> moving the manager and his family to a distant foreign loca-
> tion; the family's living pattern is not markedly changed
> with the fully developed schools, hospitals, clubs and
> beautiful environment and climate offered by El Paso. In
> fact, the cultural experience of the family is enlarged be-
> cause of the proximity of Old Mexico . . . Not the least of
> the advantages to the housewife are the international shop-
> ping facilities, as well as plentiful supply of domestic ser-
> vices available in this area.[24]

As Maria Patricia Fernández-Kelly points out, the availability
of domestic services refers to the relative ease with which
US housewives can hire the labour of undocumented Mexican
maids by paying wages below the US minimum.[25] Interestingly
enough, the cheap workers in the factories are also primarily
women.

Women in the Export Processing Zones

Outside Mexico, not all Export Processing Zones have been equally successful in enticing multinational investments. The most

spectacular success stories have been those of Shannon in Ireland, Kuoshiung in Taiwan, Bayan Lepas in Malaysia, Bataan in the Philippines and Masan in South Korea. Hong Kong and Singapore are also the talked-about successes of freeports that attracted large amounts of foreign investment (Table 3).

The proliferation of EPZs has led to a surge of competition among the host countries, each vying with the other to offer the most liberal status and excessive inducements with regard to tax

Table 3: Employment in the Export Processing Zones of selected countries

Country	Location	Employment	Year
China	Shenzen Xiamen Shantou Zhuhai	100,000	1982
Hong Kong	–	70,000	1975
Malaysia	Bayan Lepas (and 9 Other Areas)	56,000	1979
Philippines	Bataan	22,988	1982
	Three Other Areas	2,694	1981
Singapore	–	105,000	1974
South Korea	Masan (and 8 Other Areas)	120,000	1978
Taiwan	Kuoshiung (and 2 Other Areas)	77,400	1978
Sri Lanka	Katunayake	20,000	1982

Source: *Trade Unions and The Transnationals*, Brussels: International Confederation Of Free Trade Unions, March 1983.

Note: Employment in the Export Processing Zones represents only a fraction of the total employment of women in light export-oriented industries in the non-European countries. While nearly a million are employed in the zones themselves, at least three million are employed in such work outside them, mainly in the South and South-east Asian countries and in Latin America. EPZs, however, are significant as the focal points for the export-led model of development.

concessions, exchange control, terms of credit, and laxity in the implementing of labour legislation. But most of all, the countries were expected, as an OECD report stresses, to eliminate certain social costs and create a favourable 'social climate for industry'.[26] This condition involved, first and foremost, providing a docile, non-unionized labour force. It is more than a coincidence, therefore, that the new proletariat in the Export-Processing Zones shares surprisingly uniform characteristics. In most places it consists of women workers; the women tend to be between 16 and 25; they are engaged in semi-skilled or unskilled production.

Even in countries where the level of male unemployment is exceedingly high, export-led growth curiously generates employment mainly for women. This is because women are the best guarantee of that 'favourable social climate' which the host countries are expected to provide. Oriental women, with their legendary attributes of nimble fingers and docility, are the antithesis of the assertive white male workers of the West – they, therefore, provide the labour force preferred by the multinationals. The host countries shamelessly project the image of their women. As a Malaysian brochure has it:

> the manual dexterity of the oriental female is famous the world over. Her hands are small and she works with extreme care. Who, therefore, could be better qualified by nature and inheritance to contribute to the efficiency of a bench assembly production line than the oriental girl?[27]

The Royal Thai Embassy produced a similar brochure that guarantees the submissive femininity of Eastern women in an attempt to attract American investment. In Thailand, it says,

> the relationship between the employer and the employees is like that of a guardian and a ward. It is easy to win and maintain the loyalty of workers as long as they are treated with kindness and courtesy.

The facing page of the brochure offers a highly selective photo-study of Thai womanhood: giggling shyly, bowing submissively and working cheerfully on the assembly line. As Barbara Ehrenreich and Annette Fuentes comment:

Crudely put (and incidents like this do not inspire verbal delicacy), the relationship between many Third World governments and the multinational corporations is not very different from the relationship between a pimp and his customers.[28]

The 'inherent characteristics' of non-European, and particularly of oriental women, promise a grateful acceptance of low wages. In Malaysia, women workers can be hired for about US $1.50 per day. At the same time, the new proletariat in the shape of the female workforce provides the main source of foreign exchange and the hope of future industrialization from the nuclei of EPZ areas.[29] Thus it is not surprising that the state often urges the female workforce in a paternal tone to be 'good' workers in the cause of national prosperity. In an article entitled 'Why We Woo Foreign Investment', the Malaysian Deputy Prime Minister asserted:

> The government could not help the people if they refuse to realize the importance of a better economy and to be more responsible . . . workers must uphold their dignity and not cause problems that would scare away foreign investors. They should instead be more productive so that government efforts to attract investors be more successful.[30]

The stern advice indicates that the comparative advantage should be maintained. The balance of employment, as a result, understandably swings in favour of women. In most EPZ countries wages are 50 per cent lower for women than for men. In 1974, in South Korea, female workers earned on average US $0.21 per hour – less than half the male wage, which stood at US $0.43 per hour. In Taiwan, the average female wages were 58 per cent below the male average in the same year. In spite of a massive integration of women in the export-processing industries over the years, the differential, if anything, worsened. In the Masan EPZ areas in South Korea, the average wage of a woman stood at 49 per cent of the average wage of a male worker in 1974. In 1979, the figure dropped to 42 per cent. This is explained by the fact that men were consistently employed in the limited number of highly paid technical and managerial jobs, whereas women were considered 'naturally' suitable for the repetitive low-skilled assembly operations.[31] Occupational segregation and consequent wage differentials intrigued even the professional investment analysts in the West:

> 'Is the clothing industry, for example, able to pay relatively poorly in all [Third World] countries because so many of its workers are women?' asks the Economic Intelligence Unit. 'Or does its low pay tend to be acceptable to female but not to male workers?'[32]

The answer can hardly be found by pure economic analysis. It is the role of a woman as perceived by society at large that reinforces her inferior position in the job market. To that extent, Third World women share the same fate as their counterparts in the First.

To start with, it is assumed that women's employment provides a secondary rather than primary family income. Because they are not expected to support dependants they may be hired at relatively low wages. In spite of the growing phenomenon of young girls becoming the major, if not sole, breadwinners of dispossessed rural families, the myth of a woman's earnings being 'pin money' continues. A top level management consultant who specializes in advising US companies where to locate their factories said: 'The girls genuinely enjoy themselves. They're away from their families. They have spending money. They can buy motorbikes, whatever.'[33]

The reality, however, belies the claim. The great majority of women earn subsistence level incomes, whether they work for a multinational company or a locally owned factory. In the Philippines, starting wages in US-owned electronic plants are between $34 and $66 a month, and the basic cost of living is $37 a month per person. In Indonesia, the starting wages are about $7 less per month than the basic cost of living. And that basic cost of living means bare subsistence: a diet of rice, some dried fish and water, lodging in a small room occupied by four or more people.

Also, contrary to corporational belief, most women don't use their wages to buy motorbikes or other luxury items. A study of young women factory workers in Hong Kong showed that 88 per cent were turning more than half of their earnings over to their parents. In Malaysia, women electronic workers contribute 25 to 60 per cent of their wages to their families.[34] And there is growing pressure on women of both farm and lower-income backgrounds to postpone marriage and find work to help out their families. A factory girl in Bangkok or a female worker in the Katunayake zone in Sri Lanka is often the only person who can keep an entire rural family from sheer starvation.

However, the myth of a secondary earner still continues; and it is reinforced by yet another myth, that of the natural dexterity of women combined with their intellectual inferiority. Women, being dextrous, are thought ideal for assembly jobs. When asked why 90 per cent of the workers in the factory are women, the personnel manager of a maquiladora from the Mexican border answers:

> We hire mostly women because they are more reliable than men, they have finer fingers, smaller muscles and unsurpassed manual dexterity. Also, women don't get tired of repeating the same operations nine hundred times a day.[35]

Indeed, within most families, daughters are often taught skills such as sewing and needlework, which can then be extended into repetitive industrial work.[36] Nimble hands are also needed in the jobs of skilled draughtsmen and technicians – but these are areas from which female workers are totally excluded.

Another range of 'essentially female' attributes, as alleged by a former member of the Korean Central Intelligence Agency (and reported by Barbara Ehrenreich and Annette Fuentes), likewise provides major grounds for excluding women from more responsible jobs:

> Women are more susceptible than men. They are emotional and less logical . . . they are easily excited and are very reckless and do things hastily . . . management, union leaders, and city administrators find it very difficult to deal with women workers when they cause trouble. The women

weep and cry and behave exaggeratedly . . . and for men this kind of behaviour is very troubling.[37]

The image of a vulnerable, 'naturally' low-skilled community of workers is the one that the multinationals want to perpetuate. It helps them to have access to a disposable workforce, and this is essential for keeping overhead costs down.

Central to the export-oriented industrialization programme is the mobilization of a young, precariously employed proletariat whose supply can be flexible enough to meet the demand. If the global demand for clothing and electronic components declines, the companies should be able to shed labour without much trouble. It is difficult to get rid of 'the male breadwinners' without generating social tension, but it is much less of a problem with women workers. During the 1974–5 recession, for example, half of the female workers in Mexican border regions were laid off and 17,000 workers in Singapore lost their jobs. For the workers who are laid off, rehiring when production picks up again is by no means assured. New, younger workers are preferred, and, even if rehired, the experienced worker is often paid only a beginner's wage.

According to an OECD report in 1984, apprentices account for 30 to 40 per cent of the labour force employed in the clothing and electronics industries. The industrialization programme in the EPZs, therefore, is based on the availability of a workforce that is assumed to view work as a temporary interlude between childhood on the one hand and marriage and motherhood on the other.

Health hazards

The disposability of the labour force is a major precondition for success in an industry that is fraught with health hazards. In spite of its clean and clinical image, electronic assembling work, for example, brings the worker the risk of being exposed to dangerous chemicals. The list prepared by the US National Institute on Occupational Safety and Health puts electronics at the top of the list of high health risk industries. Open containers of dangerous carcinogenic acids and solvents, giving off toxic fumes, are commonplace in electronic factories. In a Hong Kong clinic survey of workers who use chemicals, 48 per cent had constant headaches, 39 per cent were often drowsy and 36 per cent had frequent sore throats.[38] At one stage of the assembly process, workers have to dip the circuits into open vats of acids. Women who do the dipping wear rubber gloves and boots, but these sometimes leak and burns are common. It is not rare for whole fingers to be lost in the process.

Electronic companies require perfect vision in new employees, but most women need glasses after a few years on the job. During the bonding process women peer through microscopes for seven to nine hours a day, attaching hair-like gold wires to silicon chips. Linda Lim in her study found that most electronic assembly workers developed eye problems after only one year of employment: 88 per cent had chronic conjunctivitis, 47 per cent became near-sighted, 19 per cent developed astigmatism. The companies, however, require 20-20 vision when they hire.[39] In most cases, companies refuse to acknowledge their responsibilities – or they treat complaints with the utmost indifference.

The working conditions in the garment and textile industry are also highly hazardous to health. Byssionosis or 'brown lung' is a common occurrence among workers. While electronic assembling work takes place in brightly lit, air-conditioned factories, the appalling conditions of work in the garment factories are often reminiscent of nineteenth-century sweatshops. The firms – generally local subcontractors to the large US and European chains such as J.C. Penney, Sears, Great Universal Stores, C & A and others – show little concern for the health of their employees. In South Korea, while the garment and textile industry helped to achieve the 'economic miracle', women workers were often packed into poorly lit rooms, where summer temperatures rise above 100 degrees Fahrenheit.

A certain amount of docility is needed to accept the health hazards that accompany such industries. In fact, one of the transnationals' major reasons for investing abroad is to seek freedom from the restrictive health and safety regulations of the West.

A letter from the Free Trade Zone of Sri Lanka

We are being made to work both day and night, like buffaloes tethered to trees. Not a single moment of the day is there for rest, both the machines and the workers. The motors of these machines become heated like furnaces. What quantity of energy is wasted of the female workers is not known. The supervisory staff and the management are never satisfied, however much we work and produce. Please focus your attention on the sufferings of the poor female workers who are being subjected to harassment and harshness by supervisors and the management.

A quantum such as is impossible for a female worker to deliver in an hour is always targeted. Fines are imposed when such quantity is not delivered on time. We are made to work even outside working hours. Even a beast will know whether it is possible to work continuously for 12 hours in the same posture seated on a four-legged stool, not even a chair is provided. . .

. . . All that we have to anticipate in the long run is to possess a debilitated and emaciated body, after exhausting what is earned, where it is earned . . .

Female Workers of . . . Garments [The name of the factory is withheld.]

Source: Voice of Women: Sri Lanka Journal for Women's Emancipation No. 4, July, 1982, 18/9, Chitra, Colombo-5, Sri Lanka.

The Western public's growing concern with industrial pollution can be neatly sidestepped by transferring production to countries that have few or no environmental regulations. The host states play the game actively: the offer of 'pollution havens' is already well advanced. In Mexico City's English-language newspapers, the State of Mexico advertises for polluters:

RELAX. WE HAVE ALREADY PREPARED THE GROUND FOR YOU. If you are thinking of fleeing from the capital because the new laws for the prevention and control of environmental pollution affect your plant, you can count on us.[40]

The host countries do their best to offer exemption from health and safety regulations. As a Malaysian health ministry doctor explained:

The government's policy is to attract investors. The first question an investor asks is: what regulations do you have, and how well do you enforce them? If he finds these two areas are weak, he comes in.[41]

The TNCs can also save substantial sums by avoiding the fringe benefits that a worker enjoys in the rich countries in the form of paid holidays and social insurance covering sickness, maternity, accident, retirement income and health care. In America, these benefits account for 36 per cent of the basic pay. These fringe benefits contribute to the total labour cost quite substantially in the developed countries; they account for about 47 per cent of the total cost in Italy, 40 per cent in France, Belgium and the Netherlands, 37 per cent in West Germany and 20 per cent in the UK. Thus the savings from avoidance of paying benefits can be substantial.

The ILO attempts to establish an international minimum standard of safety and health regulations by means of conventions and recommendations. But compliance with these is not mandatory, and standards are often below ILO levels even in developed countries. Standards may not be enforced, but even when they are, there are often provisions for exemptions. In the electronics industry, for example, there is usually a three-shift system in EPZ areas. Several countries have dispensed with the prohibition of night work for women, so that these factories can maximize production by having night shifts. In South Korea, for example,

working hours for women are set at seven per day, but if approved by the Ministry of Health and Social Affairs, even young workers, aged 13–18, are allowed to work up to nine hours per day. Overtime work for men is unregulated; for women to work the night shift is contrary to international standards, but it is possible by allowing for exceptions to the laws. While giving the external appearance of protecting the life, welfare and rights of workers, this sort of Labour Standards Law, in practice, provides a legalistic basis for gross exploitation.[42]

How women workers are used up

In Hong Kong, on 21 January 1983, women on the production line of a Japanese-owned electrical factory – Mabuchi Industry Co. Ltd. – suddenly felt unwell after inhaling an obnoxious smelling gas from a newly installed ultra-violet light attached to a printing machine. They experienced violent coughing, nose bleeds, and pain in their lungs. Three days later they again felt unwell and the management got a contractor to install a ventilation system.

The workers were instructed not to mention the incident and initially were told that if they asked for sick leave after feeling unwell from the gas leak, they would lose their good attendance bonus.

By the end of January, a total of 115 workers from Mabuchi had been hospitalized and only 33 had been discharged. Two weeks after the leak, 196 Mabuchi workers, mostly women, had sought hospital treatment and 125 were admitted.

A public seminar was held by the Industrial Health Promotion Group two weeks later to urge the authorities to release information to the public on chemicals used in Hong Kong's industries, together with details of their potential effects on health. The government's chief factory inspector responded by saying that there were enough laws governing the use of chemicals in industry.

Source: Asia Monitor Resource Centre, Hong Kong.

In other Asian countries too, the state authorities try hard to make TNC investment worthwhile. As the glossy brochure from Sri Lanka claims, the Free Trade Zone Authority can grant exemption from or modify the application of certain laws of the country, in order to offer investors a suitable and attractive incentive package.

Such exemption may even mean that firms can get away with severe infringements of the individual rights of workers without having to face legal harassment. Pregnancy tests are routinely given to potential employees to avoid the issue of maternity benefits. In India, a woman textiles worker reports that 'they do take unmarried women, but they prefer those who have had an operation'. In the Philippine Bataan Export Processing Zone, the

Mattel toy company offers prizes to those workers who undergo sterilization.

Stress and high anxiety permeate the women workers' lives, contributing to health problems. When production deadlines draw near or there are rush orders, women may be forced to work overtime for as long as 48 hours at a stretch. Management often provides pep pills and amphetamine injections to keep the women awake and working; some become permanent addicts.[43] Three to four years is the average working life of a female worker in the Export Processing Zones. A rapid turnover of labour (5 to 10 per cent a month) keeps the workforce young and productive.

Thwarting unionization is also an advantage that a permanently casual workforce gives to the corporations. It is with this end in view that married women in EPZs are employed on night shifts. As the International Confederation of Free Trade Unions' survey of the Export Processing Zones observed, married women are hired on the late night shifts so that they can do housework and care for their families during the day.[44] The system, of course, leaves very little time and energy for them to organize.

Repression of trade unions

Establishing a work pattern that leads to continuous casualization of employment is in the interest of the client states as well. Of all their enticements, the absence of trade union activity is the most attractive one they can offer the multinationals. As part of a package deal, the host government adopts various types of restrictive labour legislation. Rapid turnover of labour in such a situation pre-empts any potential trade union activities.

It is not known exactly how many women workers, out of the one million working in the zones, are organized in unions, but information from Western trade union visitors to various zones indicates that numbers are very small. In Malaysia almost all the electronic companies enjoyed 'pioneer' status, and trade unions were banned for five years in such companies. In any case, the United States' multinational electronic companies have a long record of resistance to unions. The typical attitude is summed up by Dan Nelson, Managing Director of Hewlett-Packard Malaysia, who dismisses unions in the industry as 'an unnecessary and unwelcome third party . . . which may even work against the good relationship between the management and the employees'.[45]

The Malaysian government is also anxious about the effect the unionization of electronic workers may have on the country's image. The official attitude is expressed accurately in a letter from the Labour Minister to company managers in 1980:

> The electronic industry plays an important socio-economic role in attracting foreign investment and reducing unemployment, and the question of unionization of its workers should be dealt with in a cautious manner at the present stage of the industry's development.[46]

The resultant restrictions on the right to organize among electronic workers means that virtually none of the 28,000 workers in the electronic components industry of Malaysia are unionized.

Trade unions are not very powerful in other zones either. In the Katunayake zone, Sri Lanka, no trade union is allowed. In the Philippines, draconian labour legislation, under the Marcos regime, made it difficult to have any effective unionization. The only unions that gained recognition in the Export Processing Zones were 'yellow unions' ready to co-operate with the management. With the Aquino government, rules and regulations may change, but President Marcos formulated a whole host of laws, orders and decrees that banned all forms of assembly and meeting without government permits. Suspected subversives could be arrested without trial. The notorious Cayetano Bill included severe penalties for violation of anti-strike laws.

Industries within EPZs are explicitly identified as belonging to those affecting the 'national interest'. In the event of labour disputes, the Ministry of Labour and Employment may issue a back-to-work order and impose compulsory arbitration. Even where legislation permits labour organization in principle, it is often prevented by companies with the tacit or active support of the government. In fact, in order to maintain a 'harmonious' relationship with labour, the zones are carefully segregated geographically in almost all countries in which they are located. In smaller countries, such as Singapore, Taiwan and South Korea, such geographic segregation of an EPZ is not feasible; there the government-backed trade union is used both for disciplining and encouraging greater productivity among workers. The workers' right to negotiate in these countries is severely limited.

The harsh treatment of labour movements itself sows seeds of discontent and rebellion. The OECD report *Investing in Free Export Processing Zones* comments anxiously:

> In practice, it is not at all certain that such measures will really be to the investor's advantage in the long run. In fact in the case of a serious crisis the absence of institutional mechanisms for concertation may provoke a brutal rupture of social peace.[47]

Maintenance of social peace in this situation is partly guaranteed by the nature of the industrialization process, which relies mainly on cheap, disciplined female labour to manufacture light consumer goods for the world market. The strategy stands in sharp contrast with the early industrialization process of the Latin American countries such as Mexico, Brazil, Argentina and Uruguay, where industrial structuring was geared to a greater diversification, in response to declining primary export prices during the depression of the 1930s. The import-substitution policy there relied on traditional and heavy industries, and was associated with relatively high-wage, high-skill and male-intensive employment. The result has been a vigorous labour movement. This is in spite of the fact that southern Latin American labour movements have, especially since the mid-1960s, been confronted by highly repressive, military-backed regimes whose only Asian parallel has been in Korea.

Yet, despite more repressive regimes, labour movements in Latin America, organized around male workers employed in import-substitution industries, have displayed far greater vigour than movements in the so-called Asian 'gang of four' (Singapore, Taiwan, Hong Kong and South Korea). For in these, industrialization relied on low-wage, low-skill, female-intensive employment which provided, apart from other advantages, a good foundation for 'harmonious' labour relations.[48]

The success model of the Asian 'gang of four' is being increasingly emulated by other developing countries. The limited extent of a labour movement in these countries, where manufacturing employment is high, can be explained by the preponderance of short-term employees, who get physically too exhausted to stay in the workforce for longer than three or four years. A correlation between the extent of light manufacturing industry and the weakness of the labour movement is not fortuitous; the reliance on female-intensive employment for the world market factories is part of an overall strategy to contain existing or potential trade union movements in the client states (Table 4).

Table 4: Light industries dominate the economy of the Asian Gang of Four
Manufacturing employment in selected industries (per cent)[a]

	Heavy	Light
Argentina (1979)	49	3
Brazil (1976)[b]	32	23
Mexico (1980)	35	20
Singapore (1980)	23	43
South Korea (1978)	17	42
Hong Kong (1980)	5	62
Taiwan (1980)	19	38

Source: [a] ILO, 1982
         [b] The Economist Intelligence Unit (1981)

Militarization of the state

The careful structuring of industries is only a part of the guaranteed social peace. Increasing political and military links between the home and the host country promise the environment most favourable for multinational investments. In fact, with total assets of $760 billion, the multinational companies in the US can exert considerable pressure on their government to give military and political aid to 'friendly' host states. Other Western powers soon follow the American example.

Militarization of the host states has been one of the major consequences of the export-led growth in Third World countries. They can hardly afford to lose the 'good worker' image in an environment where there is cut-throat competition to attract the corporations. The patriarchal values of the state often collude, therefore, with those of the multinationals, to augment the militarization of Third World countries which have EPZ areas. Military expenditure per head in these countries is staggeringly high, to enable them to stage what Herbert Marcuse would call 'preventive counter-revolutions', in order to keep the workforce, especially the women, in their place.

It is not an accident, therefore, that export-oriented industrialization has been successful only in those countries whose far-reaching economic links with the West (and with Japan) have been reinforced by strong political bonds. Multinationals looked for political stability in their client states; but they also needed support from ruling political groups in those states against domestic opposition. Hong Kong's colonial status and the political-military client status of Singapore, South Korea and Taiwan vis-à-vis the West played an essential part in their attracting TNC investments. There is also a consistent record of military aid from the metropolis to those Third World governments that are capitalist, politically repressive, and not striving for economic independence. The result is that export-oriented growth has almost invariably led to further militarization. Thailand has been ruled by a military junta since 1976. Singapore's dictator Lee Kuan Yew took power in 1959, repressing students, unionists, leftists and the media. The bloody coup in Indonesia in 1965, with the help of the political police (KOPKAMTIB), ushered in the regime of Suharto, who placed strict controls on labour organizing and banned all strikes. Malaysia, as we have seen, had labour ordinances restricting unionization; the unions which exist are weak and ineffective. The Marcos dictatorship in the Philippines was cited by Amnesty International for its consistent record of human rights violations and repressions. Military aid from the US to these five countries must be reckoned in hundreds of millions of dollars: the Philippines alone received 140 million dollars in 1982. Although the political picture there has changed very recently, it is too soon to say how the military links will be affected. In general, however, such military aid has been openly welcomed by the host states.

A distorted pattern of development that relies primarily on the employment of very young and female labour in the light export industries does little to alleviate the problems of growing landlessness, male unemployment, and often spiralling inflation in Third World countries. In the Philippines, for example, most of the operations of the Marcos government's coercive forces were focused on the New People's Army (NPA) insurgents in the rural areas of Luzon and Samar, and on the Muslim peasants, dispossessed by the multinational agribusiness, on the southern island of Mindanao. As the expenditure on military and police expansion increased, it deprived the Marcos government of resources for its health, education and social security programmes, that could improve the living conditions of the workers. Instead, the government had to buy more and more military and police equipment overseas, and that in turn increased the need of foreign currency earnings that the cheap female labour in EPZ areas could bring.

The trend towards increased militarization is likewise visible in other South-east Asian countries that depend on young female labour for their internationally competitive industrialization. At the beginning of 1981, the Malaysian government announced that expenditure on both its police and military personnel would increase. Under the 1976–81 Third Malaysian plan, defence received M $1.5 million; under the Fourth Malaysian plan the budget jumped to M $9.8 million. The Malaysian army grew from 52,500 in 1978 to 90,000 in 1980, and was scheduled to expand even further; the paramilitary arm of the Malaysian police was expected to grow from 58,000 in 1981 to 120,000 in 1985. This growth occurs as US, German, Dutch and Japanese firms are being encouraged to set up factories in Malaysia. To quote Cynthia Enloe:

Militarization is pursued by male elites when they are nervous, insecure in their grasp on power. In the Philippines – as in South Korea, Taiwan, Hong Kong, Singapore, Indonesia, Malaysia and Thailand – governmental insecurity stems from a keen awareness that state maintenance rests on 19-year-old women factory workers and on the gender ideologies of dexterity, docility and family obedience that enable foreign and local entrepreneurs to mobilize them. Patriarchy alone – without police and military reinforcement – is seen by elites as inadequate to sustain the kind of discipline they need in order to reassure foreign investors that their societies are 'good bets' for profitable investment.[49]

Against this backdrop of militarization, the multinationals formulate appropriate management strategies to dispel potential organization by the women workers.

Corporate management and the family: a happy complicity

Strategies for defusing potential organized protests are varied, and are formulated in the context of the specific labour conditions of the host country. But the stress is invariably on the paternalistic image, where the management plays the role of a strict but benevolent father. Fairness of attitude is often suggested by encouraging the workers to organize workers' councils, where they are given the opportunity to air their grievances publicly. The idea is to convince the workers that the management is indeed willing to co-operate, if given a proper forum. In reality, the councils have very little influence on changing management policies. However, forming such councils serves a purpose useful to the management – it diverts the workers' attention and energy from union activities.

Another method is to cultivate an individual relationship between management and workers by encouraging workers to take problems directly to the personnel officer. If the problem gets handled satisfactorily at the personal level, the worker will fail to see that it arises out of problematic conditions in the structure of employment, the redress of which demands concerted group action.

Reinforcing the sexual stereotypes of women workers dependent on men for approval and support is the most common method of ensuring docility. Beauty contests are an integral part of factory life, with each company sending its beauty queen to the yearly 'Miss Free Trade Zone' contest. Cosmetics are sold in company-sponsored cosmetic classes, and women workers are encouraged to compete against one another as sex objects. Company-sponsored recreational activities are designed to divert workers' demands for job improvements. A US plant manager in Malaysia says, 'We have developed recreation to a technique, with sewing classes, singing competitions and sports events.' In personnel newsletters or company publications, it is extremely rare to find articles on national or community issues. Instead they include sexist humour, advice columns, articles on family life and on appearance, reinforcing the concept of women's dependence on men.

If the workers' organized protests are being thwarted by the employers' relentless assertion of so-called feminine attributes, harmony on the factory floor is being sought through the ideology of family life. Women workers are expected to reproduce the same obedient behaviour to factory managers as is expected of a good daughter to her father. Messages carrying slogans about the family and family spirit can reach the worker through loudspeaker broadcasts in the factory, posters, personal contacts with managers and official publications. Typical are such slogans as, 'Catch on to the [company] family spirit and build a good future for you and your family.' International business strategies are explained to the workers, to create a feeling of belonging to the larger organization and a sense of identity with the corporate interests.

The family analogy is easy to maintain, as those in the position of power in the factory are invariably men. As the manager of Fairchild's Indonesian plant explained, 'What we are doing resembles a family system in which I am not just the manager but also a father to all of those here in Fairchild.'[50]

The thrust of the management policy is to perpetuate the

'desirable' image of a subservient and dutiful daughter in their female workers. To this end, the multinationals shamelessly take advantage of the sexual power-relationships at home. A lot of women are deliberately recruited by multinationals as daughters whose fathers have a stake in their working. The men, who want their daughters' (or sisters') pay, will allow poor wages and working conditions to prevail as long as the managers supervise the girls and keep them 'pure'. There is an amazingly ready alliance between personnel managers and parents, especially fathers. As Cynthia Enloe says, it is a happy complicity.[51]

Male opposition to women organizing: a Sri Lankan woman speaks

In Sri Lanka it's harder because trade union access to Free Trade Zones is restricted and talking about it is discouraged. High unemployment means jobs are sought after and the workers want to keep them – they are threatened if they join a trade union. They can't participate in work stoppages because of lost pay and in the end negotiate with management themselves. There are phoney 'workers' councils' but really it's management. If there are no trade unions then they must organize outside the factory at the Women's Centre to let them meet women who have already organized – some Free Trade Zones have trade unions outside the zone. Women must share experiences and organize together. Because Free Trade Zones are 90% women, then women must be the organizers. Men are not interested in the same demands, being already higher paid. They sold out in the end and allowed women to be prevented from taking 'skilled' jobs e.g. cutting. They didn't want to meet with women and would humiliate them by making them kneel on the floor, like punishment at school, preventing them from working.

For trying to organize, women would be sacked on the pretext that they were not able to meet artificially high production demands. Now women are agreeing production limits amongst themselves to prevent this happening. Men are not interested in what women say, so women must organize themselves.

A speaker from Sri Lanka.

Source: Women Working Worldwide Conference in London, 24 April 1983.

While the state tries to crush women on strike

Under emergency laws in Sri Lanka, it is illegal for more than five persons to gather in one place. Nevertheless, 700 striking women workers of Polytex Garments Colombo assembled across from their factory in December 1982. *'We all assembled in a private garden 100 yards from the factory. By 7 a.m., the police came and asked us to move . . . we said we were conducting a peaceful strike and did not intend to leave. The police came a second time and threatened to shoot us, aiming guns at our chests. We sat up, stretched out our hands and told them to go ahead and shoot. The police who had expected us to run were completely taken aback. Instead of shooting us, they turned their guns skyward and shot into the air. No one moved from where they were. Then we were teargassed and assaulted; 18 women received injuries, four of our union leaders arrested. This situation was a totally new experience to a majority of the women, yet we resolutely withstood the attack and became more determined to fight and win our demands.'*

Source: W. Chapkis and C. Enloe (eds), *Of Common Cloth. Women in the Global Textile Industry*, Transnational Institute: Amsterdam 1983.

This reproduction of family life on the factory floor takes away from girls one of the major motives behind wanting to be a factory-worker: the desire for a life that promises freedom from patriarchal oppression in a rural feudalistic society. In fact waged employment rarely represents a liberation for a Third World woman – on the contrary, it often brings an added hazard of sexual exploitation. 'We call our company "motel",' says a worker at Mattel in the Bataan Export Processing Zone in the Philippines, 'because we are often told to lie down or be laid off.'[52] In the maquiladoras of the Mexican Border Industrialization Programme, Fernández-Kelly observed that women often find themselves in situations where they have to resort to their sexuality in order to gain access to, or stability of, employment. In the job market, 'sexual behaviour among maquiladora workers is frequently more than a moral issue. It is a vivid expression of the feeble political position that women have in society.'[53]

The possibility of sexual exploitation in the factory increases the stigma attached to 'factory girls' in a traditional rural society: it makes them unfit for marriage, as sexual purity is highly prized in such societies. For a woman thrown out of work on the assembly line at an early age, prostitution is often the only form of livelihood left. In this new role, too, she becomes an important source of foreign exchange for the country, as tourism becomes part of the overall strategy of export-led growth.

Prostitution and sex-tourism

For 1973, the South Korean government had set itself the goal of an annual number of 500,000 tourists and 100 million dollars from the tourist trade, but the planned target was exceeded even before June that year. At the heart of this increasing tourist trade lies the Kisaeng tour, specially geared to the Japanese business-man. As a 'morale booster', Japanese companies reward their outstanding branch managers and salesmen with all-expenses-paid tours of South Korea's brothels: one or two nights of Kisaeng parties. The 'comparative advantage' of South Korea is beyond question. Chartered tours of two nights and three days cost no more than $200 and a tour of three nights and four days costs only $250. The benefits to South Korea are also substantial. A typical Kisaeng rate for single customers is $60 a night in Seoul and $50 in Pusan. Extra foreign exchange is also earned through tips and additional travel expenses. Special discount rates are given for large group Kisaeng parties, and if more than 30 members sign up, two men are allowed to attend free of charge. But they spend generously. Apart from the standard fee of $50 or $60 each, Japanese men often spend $150 or more for other services. So if jets, each carrying 300 Japanese tourists, land in South Korea every day, it leads to a large annual revenue of foreign exchange. For the host country, prostitution really pays.

In South Korea, prostitution-tourism is a part of the planned economic development. Prospective Kisaeng are given lectures by a male university professor on the crucial role of tourism in South Korea's economy before they get their prostitution lic-ences. And South Korean ministers have praised 'the sincerity of girls who have contributed to their fatherland's economic de-velopment'.[54]

These sex-tours have earned Japanese businessmen the nick-name 'sex animals'. The image is so strong that in South Korea women find it difficult to believe that Japanese tourists can have any other reason for visiting. When a group of Japanese recently went to South Korea to do research on the underground resist-ance during the era of Japanese colonialism between 1905 and 1945, they caused a stir at a country inn by refusing to receive prostitutes. The young men were reported to the local police as being suspicious characters masquerading as Japanese![55]

Sex-tours provide the second or third most important source of foreign exchange in Thailand and the Philippines. But not all the tourists are Japanese. Americans, Europeans and Australians are regular visitors, though they are less likely to move in groups. And as in South Korea, the tourist industry flourishes on the use of women, with the explicit connivance of the government. In Thailand, prostitution, strictly speaking, is illegal, but the mas-sage parlours that abound in the city offer their services with the protection and help of the local police. Understandably the ILO study on the subject – *From Peasant Girls to Bangkok Masseuses* – ironically and candidly reports that out of hundreds, 'There is one massage parlour in Bangkok which is especially famous. It offers only massage.'[56]

In the Philippines, as in Thailand, prostitution is illegal, but the government encourages the use of 'hospitality girls' in tourism, which is a euphemism for prostitution. There are about 120 flesh shops in Manila's tourist belt; 21 are recommended by the Ministry of Tourism and licensed by the City Hall. Each shop has 80–200 hospitality girls – girls employed by licensed tour agencies. Typically, a large Japanese, European or American operator will advertise a 'package' tour to the Philippines in co-operation with a Manila agent. The deal includes everything from shopping to hotel and women, who are either chosen from pictures or selected in one of the large clubs.

Men pay, on average, $60 for one night with a woman, but the woman herself receives very little of this money. The following is a rough breakdown: club owner $25; tour operator $15; local guide $10; Japanese guide $10. The woman receives between $4.25 and $5.75 from the owner's share. According to the findings of A. Lin Neumann, at times they do not even get that much, because the club management imposes fines for improper dress, smoking, drinking, tardiness and other arbitrary infractions.[57] The working life of prostitutes is not very long either. The level of violence and drug usage is high, especially in the US military bases. When asked what happens to women as they grow older, one Catholic nun who works among them commented, 'Many of them die before they grow old because of drugs.' Other women are reduced to performing lewd acts in the clubs after they lose their sexual desirability.[58]

The travel brochures in West Germany and Holland advertise the sex-tours with allurements, promising 'a meeting with the most beautiful young Eastern creatures (age 16 to 24 years) in a soft and sexy surrounding and in the seductive and tropical night of the exotic paradise'. The sex-tours also offer additional services: the purchase of women, arranged by travel agencies such as Neckermann's and Christoffel's in West Germany, with the co-operation of their South Asian tourist and business counterparts. Various 'marriage bureaux' in Hong Kong, Singapore, Japan, West Germany and Holland have sprung up to make it easy for the client to choose his future 'wife' from illustrated colour catalogues in the ease and comfort of his own home. An enamoured client can buy a woman outright for DM 20,000; later on, the woman, his property, can be hired out to pimps in the West.

Prostitution-tourism in Third World countries is becoming scandalously popular in Europe. The men who take these tours come from all walks of life. An airline which carries a planeload every Sunday from Amsterdam to Bangkok has become commonly known, for understandable reasons, as the 'gonorrhoea express'.[59]

The experiences of women thrown out of the global assembly line in the Latin American and Caribbean countries are similar to those of women in South-east Asia. As they acquire no skill or training in the factories of the international corporations, many of them, especially if they are heads of households, end up in prostitution. In this new profession, non-European women in Asia and Latin America suffer from double exploitation – as

women and as blacks. The Western sex-tourists need not suffer
from inhibitions with black women; they are different from their
own women and hence need not be treated with restraint. Ironically, Japanese men too feel racially superior to other Asians; the
behaviour of Japanese 'sex-animals', therefore, is no different
from that of white foreigners.

The tourist trade flourishes on the myth of docile black
women. The differences between non-white females and their
liberated white counterparts are continually emphasized in the
enticements to sex-tours. The travel advertisements themselves,
often in sex magazines, stress that 'the man who has difficulty in
establishing a relationship here [in the West], in Bangkok can
choose among hundreds of young women who, for a tiny
amount, will make him feel like Don Juan'. Similarly, in Latin
America, black girls are supposed to be born to please: to a Col-
ombian girl, 'a man is a man, he is never too old, never too short,
never too fat, never too thin, never too tall and never too ugly'.[60]
A male press writer from Frankfurt rhapsodizes about Asian
women who are 'without desire for emancipation but full of
warm sensuality and the softness of velvet'.[61]

The futility of export-oriented industrialization

The increase in militancy among women workers in non-
European countries in the last five years, however, has undermined the myth of submissive oriental and black women. The
increased militancy itself has been the result of the unfulfilled
promises that export-oriented industrialization offered. One
does not need the voices of radical thinkers to point out the
failure of development plans around multinational investment in
the Export Processing Zones. A recent OECD report, *Investing
in Free Export Processing Zones*, abounds with evidence of dis-
illusion.[62]

The first disillusionment is with the host country's hope of ac-
quiring skills and know-how, generally known as the promise of
technology-transfer. The report comments:

There is reason to be sceptical as to the effectiveness and

significance of the transfer made within EPZs [since they] only favour routine activities . . . as in the case of the electronic component industry [they offer] little chance for improvement, calling on unskilled labour which can adapt to the jobs created after only a few days' training. What is more, the specialized nature of the tasks prevents any skills acquired, however slight, being of use in other sectors of production.

In some of the newly industrialized countries, such as South Korea and Singapore, there have been some moves towards technology-intensive production. But there too, the benefits of technology-transfer from multinational investments have remained a thorny problem. The *Financial Times* report on South Korea in 1985 documents this:

Korea's complaint about Japan . . . is Japan's denial of advanced technology to Korean manufacturers, allegedly for fear of a so-called 'boomerang effect' – the possibility that low-cost Korean competition will undercut Japanese dominance of certain high-technology markets.[63]

Although the hope of learning-by-doing remained unfulfilled in the client countries, the investment by foreign companies in EPZ areas could be justified on the grounds of increased exports and foreign exchange earnings. Indeed, according to United Nations Commission on Trade, Aid and Development (UNCTAD) estimates, the EPZs have had a considerable role in the total generation of extra revenue in a number of countries. However, even in those countries, the strain on foreign and domestic currency reserves resulting from the cost of providing services, facilities, infrastructure, energy and building, often outweighs the benefits of extra earnings. From 1973 to 1982, the firms in the Bataan zone of the Philippines earned a sum of $82 million in foreign exchange, yet the sum hardly offset the expense of building the zone at a total cost of $192 million. In fact, instead of making a net contribution to the country's financial flow, the foreign companies often use up domestic capital by borrowing inside the country. As Peter Warr of the Australian National University has shown, the estimated loss to the Philippines from domestic borrowing by foreign firms in the zone is itself large enough to cancel all the gain from employment generation and foreign exchange earnings.[64]

In addition, the import of a very high proportion of raw materials and intermediate goods invariably means that the net contribution of TNC investment is much less than the gross contribution implied by the increase in the value of exports. The International Labour Organization-Asian Regional Team for Employment Promotion (ILO-ARTEP) survey found that in the Katunayake zone in Sri Lanka, in the case of electrical appliances, the value of imports of raw materials was 163 per cent of exports. In Singapore, American semiconductor firms bought less than 10 per cent of the material inputs locally.[65] The distinguishing feature of the multinational companies' investment in the Free Trade Zone areas in all countries is that it hardly creates any linkage with the domestic economy. As the OECD report succinctly comments, 'Not only is intra-firm supply of inputs held to be a guarantee of quality and exact compliance with standards, it also permits an advantageous transfer-pricing policy.'[66] The practice of transfer-pricing allows TNCs to show a profit or loss at will in a given country, by adjusting the prices on intra-company sales; in this way the overall corporate tax liability can be kept low. The TNCs' tax liability in the client states is, in any case, minimal; concessions such as 100 per cent tax-free profit repatriation in fact mean a heavy drain on the country's reserves and resources. This is especially so as the profits in the Free Trade Zone areas are generally high.

What benefits do the countries get from the investment of the transnational corporations? The only benefit seems to be the creation of employment of a rather vulnerable and unbalanced nature – above all, of young women, who are willing to work at high intensity and at an extremely low wage rate. As soon as the tax-holidays run out in the host country, or the technology changes, or the workers show signs of militancy, the TNCs move away to a greener pasture. For this precarious kind of employment, women in the client countries are expected to pay a high price in terms of health hazards, social disruptions and a quasi-military discipline at the factory level. Their career progression from factory floor to massage parlour and brothel does not seem too desirable either.

The demise of export-led growth is already in sight. To quote *International Labour Reports*, January–February 1986:

> The Malaysian government, which had hoped that electronics would provide the base for a new era of industrial development in the country, is now telling electronic workers to go back to the paddy fields. Thousands of workers, all over South-east Asia, most of them women, are being laid off by the subsidiaries of Japanese and US transnational companies without consultation and frequently with wages owing to them. Retrenchment is being put down not only to a fall in demand but also to new technology.
>
> A South-east Asian worker using manual equipment can wire as many as 120 integrated circuits to the frames in an hour. By contrast an automated machine can wire 640 circuits an hour and one worker can monitor eight machines at a time. In Malaysia alone, 10,000 electronic workers have lost their jobs this year, and Singapore, after years of dazzling performance, is experiencing a *negative* rate of growth this year for the first time.

The World Bank and the IMF

However, this type of insecure development pattern is exactly what has had the blessing of international agencies such as the World Bank, the International Monetary Fund (IMF) and the United Nations Industrial Development Organization (UNIDO). Of these three, the role of UNIDO has been relatively passive. It provided technical assistance and carried out feasibility studies for planning and implanting EPZs at the request of developing countries. The role of the other two agencies can hardly be deemed neutral or apolitical.

In general, the World Bank's loans to Third World countries are conditional upon their compliance with the Bank's own economic philosophy, which strongly advocates the elimination of import tariffs, which protect domestic industry but hamper the granting of tax-holidays to foreign investors and the creation of Free Trade Zones. The Sri Lankan garment industry, for example, was set up under these conditions, with a $20 million loan and advice from the World Bank. The result was that young women workers got jobs there at a global low level of $5 for a six-day working week.

The IMF, a sister institution of the World Bank, plays an equally active role in providing an 'open' economy which facilitates multinational investments. The IMF, which is a major source of short-term finance for governments with balance-of-payment problems, is a net lender to the Third World. The IMF's loans, however, are contingent upon the acceptance of the standard 'stabilization' programme that includes control of wages, abolition of price controls and subsidies, and most of all, dismantling of any policies, such as import and export controls, that are unfavourable to foreign investors.

The creation of an open economy and the dynamics of export-led growth have been given an extra boost from a new source of funding since the 1970s. This came from private commercial banks in the West – the deposit banks of 'petrodollars' from the OPEC countries. After the increase in oil prices of the early 1970s, there was a massive rise of so-called 'petrodollars' which could not be profitably invested in the advanced capitalist countries, beset with the problems of structural adjustment and recession. So the banks found, to quote Teresa Hayter,

> a 'sink-hole' for their money in the Third World and Eastern Europe, in the shape of governments eager and willing to invest it or at least take it, in Mexico, Brazil, Argentina, Poland, Romania, the Philippines, South Korea. At the Annual Meeting of the World Bank and the IMF, Finance Ministers were pursued by bankers offering them money with no strings attached. Just sign on the napkin, they were reported to have said amid the extravagant abundance of their parties.[67]

The process came to be known as 'recycling' of the OPEC surplus of petrodollars.

The programme of export-led growth in the newly developing countries provided a profitable ground of investment for the multinational financial institutions. The size of the loans and the speed with which they were lent were dazzling. In 1970, the private banks' loans to developing countries stood at about $7.73 billion. By 1981, they were lending $22 billion, of which Mexico and Brazil alone accounted for nearly $9 billion. The total debt of the Third World countries stood at $180 billion by 1981. Brazil and Mexico together accounted for a total debt of $79 billion. In the 1970s, such massive increases in the debt burden did not matter; real rates of interest on the debt were very low or even negative (below the rate of inflation), and the debt crisis was not yet a problem. In fact, the bonanza of growth that the injection of new money created in some countries in the South was praised internationally. The private banks were thought to be doing a brilliant job in recycling the surplus OPEC money to the countries that could use it profitably.[68]

The euphoria was to be short-lived. Because of rising interest rates, by 1979 Third World debt service charges rose by $7.5 billion. The average interest rate was 7 per cent in 1975, but close to 18 per cent by 1981. It was the spiralling defence expenditure in the US, and a consequent deficit in the budget, which fuelled a steady rise in interest rates, adding billions to Third World debt service charges. By 1981 the net outflow of private, mainly bank, funds from developing countries to the North reached a massive sum of $21 billion. The way things are going now, the big borrowers will inevitably need a constant supply of new money just to keep paying the interest – a bondage that would destroy any hope for future growth and development. Any painfully achieved increases in the exports of the debtor countries now go straight into debt servicing rather than into imports.[69]

In this situation the stringent prescription of the IMF magnifies the plight of the working class – especially of women and children – in the countries it is supposedly aiding. Debtor governments, in an attempt to reschedule their debts, are now faced with going to the IMF for further loans and accepting the conditions attached to the receipt of this money. The stabilization policy of the IMF invariably means coercing governments to 'put their houses in order'. This involves a severe deflationary policy, leading to a drastic reduction in investment, wages and food subsidies, so that resources can be diverted back to the lending banks. As a result of the standard IMF prescriptions, four million people lost their jobs in Mexico, prices of bread, tortilla and other necessary goods doubled, public expenditure was slashed and wages declined. In Brazil, the IMF demanded an annual reduction of 2 per cent in wages; as a result, between 1981 and 1982 the number of Brazilians earning less than half the minimum wage increased by a third, to over 10 million.[70] Not surprisingly, desperate crowds resorted to raiding supermarkets for basic foodstuffs.

Similar pictures emerged with chilling predictability in every debtor country. Austere measures adopted by Bolivia in order to obtain a loan from the IMF have caused the price of daily bread to the poor to double overnight. Kerosene, the fuel of the poor for light and cooking, went up 300 per cent in 1984. Public transport in urban and rural areas rocketed between 40 and 100 per cent in the same year. By the end of March 1985, the annual rate of inflation in Bolivia had reached 8,216 per cent, or 22.5 per cent for every day of the year.[71] Although in theory a neutral institution, the IMF has successfully shifted the burden of bailing out the private banks from taxpayers in the North to the poor in the South.[72] Even in the debtor countries, the rich remain unaffected; but it is the poor who pay the price of the reckless lending and spending of yesteryear. There are now 20 million abandoned and undernourished children in Brazil, a country that has the resources to feed not only all its own children but also millions in other countries.[73]

The Third World debt crisis was made serious by the very nature of export-oriented industrialization. From the very beginning it was critically dependent on the willingness of the international community to support a reasonable climate of free trade. But by the late 1970s, the favourable external conditions, which had encouraged so many Third World countries to embark on this particular path of development, had disappeared. The recession and inflation were choking off substantial growth in the major markets of Europe, the US and Japan; and EOI as a strategy was directly threatened by the protectionist wave in rich countries.

The bitter experience of experiments with export-led development did not stop the World Bank from prescribing the same strategy to other non-European countries. In fact, with shrinking markets, rising protectionism and rapid changes in technology, the exports of one country can grow only if another country's exports decline. This results in competing countries' greater efforts to reduce the cost of the key factor of production, i.e. labour. The experience often confirms the fear, to quote Walden Bello,

> that the World Bank's primary intention in . . . the Third World was not to promote industrial growth. It was to satisfy the multinational firms' need for cheap labour and the advanced metropolitan economies' craving for cheap light manufactured goods by pitting one Third World country's working class against the others in a race toward the bottom line of survival.[74]

The Bank defends its policy passionately: 'Our job is to help eliminate poverty. It is not our responsibility if the multinationals come and offer such low wages. It is the responsibility of the governments.'[75] Unfortunately it is one of the conditions as well as the consequences of the multinational investment that the host government itself becomes an ally of the transnational corporations. It is not surprising, therefore, that it is the poor – among whom women workers tend to be the poorest – who are now taking control of their working lives, through uprisings and organization, in the Third World.

Third world women organize

The newsletter of the British-owned Intercontinental Garments Manufacturing Company benignly states: 'Regarding Filipino women labour, most foreign manufacturing experts have this to say: they are very adaptable, of good temperament and generally quite cheerful. This is why they are much sought-after as garment-makers.' Ironically, it is these young and inexperienced women in the Philippines and other Third World countries who have effectively shattered the myth of compliant female workers and have produced one of the most highly organized and militant workforces in Asia and Latin America. The exploitative jobs in the factories of Free Trade Zones have led to a new solidarity among women workers, often leading to a wider struggle for independence and distributive justice. As Begum Jahanara, 28-year-old vice-president of the Bangladesh Garment Workers' Federation, stresses:

> Working for the export market has given 150,000 young Muslim women [in Bangladesh] the chance to be economically independent temporarily, and thereby to defy the taboos of an orthodox society. The jobs are exploitative, at an average wage of £12.00 per month; but still these are jobs. Look what confidence the wage-earning has given to these women. They are organizing themselves, demanding better conditions of work and higher wages. When you think that a large number of them have run away from the oppression of married life, because they could not bring a big enough dowry to their husband's home! These jobs have been catalysts for a bigger struggle for women's independence.[76]

Unfortunately, for many young non-European and black women, assembly-line work provides the only escape route from poverty for themselves and their extended family. Their struggle inevitably is centred on improving their wages and conditions of work. In spite of government repression and corporate threats to move to another country with more peaceful social conditions, more and more women are organizing themselves to fight for greater control over their working lives. Annette Fuentes and Barbara Ehrenreich have documented a number of such struggles in their monograph *Women in the Global Factory. The Plight of Asian Workers in Electronics*, published by the Christian Conference of Asia in Hong Kong, likewise describes various important uprisings at the beginning of the 1980s by women in the global assembly line of South-east Asia. Indeed, the strength of women's organizations in channelling their protest is being shown continuously in industrial unrest. It was ironic, to quote Cynthia Enloe, that 'the export-processing zone was defined around a domestic ideology with the women in secure areas living in greatly supervised dorms. But it turned out to be a place from where women's solidarity grows.'[77]

The industrial dispute at Control Data Korea (a subsidiary of the US-based Control Data Corporation) in 1981–2 marked a new and more precarious phase in the struggle of women workers. This is a phase that is characterized by fresh changes in techniques of production, that can make the cheap labour of women itself redundant. Demand for improved wages and working conditions in this situation can easily be counteracted by the management with a shutdown of offshore plants. In response to workers' militant demands, the Control Data management announced that the development of photolithography-produced computer chips had made the labour-intensive assembly work of the Seoul Plant quite unnecessary.[78]

Fights for security of work and for a reasonable wage level in the new situation are taking different and more intense forms. The 'sympathy' or 'indignation' strikes that have taken place in the Bataan EPZ in the last three years indicate a new development in this direction. Essentially, the 'sympathy' strikes involve a zone-wide stoppage for workers, irrespective of the company they work for. The very first of these strikes took place in June 1982, when 200 workers walked out of the Japanese-owned Interasia Company in protest against forced overtime and an increased workload. As the striking workers were brutally attacked by the zone police, sympathy and solidarity grew among the fellow-workers, culminating in a mass stoppage in the zone involving 20,000 women in 23 factories. This unprecedented solidarity alarmed the authorities, who forced the management to negotiate and make concessions. The sympathy strike also broadened the organizational base of the labour movement in the zone. Out of the dispute was formed AMB-A-BALA (Bataan Alliance of Labour Association), whose task was to co-ordinate union activity in the zone and maintain a sense of solidarity among workers.[79]

With increased organizational strength, mass stoppages took

place twice in the following two years. In 1983, when workers in the British-owned Astec Electronics went on strike for union recognition, battle-trained marines joined the police to break the strike. But with the ability of the workers to bring every factory in the zone to a halt, management again had to yield. In the summer of 1984, Bataan experienced yet another successful mass stoppage, over the acceptance of union officials in Interasia. Thus by January 1985, to quote the International Labour Report, 'a zone which the government boasted would never have a strike had been hit by three general strikes in three years and involving up to 20,000 workers!'[80]

The experience in the Philippines shows the potential of organizing workers in the zones against even the most powerful companies. With a show of solidarity, it is not impossible to have negotiations for improving the workers' conditions even in the face of military repression. But the experience also highlights the limited effectiveness of such moves in the long term. The closure of factories in the zone is already quite dramatic. Between 1982 and 1985 the workforce declined by a quarter and the number may dwindle even further. In a country where the level of unemployment and the consequent poverty are high, such a rapid decline in jobs is bound to have serious implications.

The dilemma that women workers face in this situation has forced them to rethink their own strategies. In the Philippines, especially since 1984, this has involved broadening the organizational base of women in a framework that transcends the demand for redress of immediate economic grievances on the factory floor. Women workers' struggles are now seen as a part of a nationwide women's movement – GABRIELA – that pledges to fight for economic self-reliance and for a free and just society. An umbrella organization of more than 70 women's networks, the movement aims to adhere to the principles expressed in its name: General Assembly Binding (Women) for Reforms, Integrity, Equality, Leadership and Action. This name is also designed to recall that of Gabriela Silany, the first Filipino General to lead a rebellion against the Spaniards in the eighteenth century. In her spirit, the new GABRIELA movement aims to wage action against the domination of TNCs and US imperialism. To

The women's movement and the social change in the Philippines

'Because we are living under a repressive US-backed regime the national question has been given priority over the women's question both in the underground and in the legal opposition. Times are changing now. Women are beginning to mobilize themselves as women. There's no question of a separatist, anti-male movement. Men and women are fighting together in the general struggle to change society. But women are no longer sitting back and letting women's issues be considered secondary ones in the movement.

'The whole issue of child care (for example) hasn't even been touched yet by the unions. It's really hard for women workers and it's almost impossible for women with children to go to meetings or organize other workers.

'It's a problem to get men to help women,' adds Minda. 'We are still studying how to convince husbands of their responsibilities in parenting. All our solutions are individual ones as yet. I was married, but my husband and I separated after our child was born. We were both full-time labour organizers. All he would do is organize. I had to do everything for the baby. We separated over this.'

Source: Marilee Karl, 'The New Women's Movement In the Philippines', *Spare Rib*, August 1983.

this end, the movement is trying to 'develop a broad, comprehensive and deeper involvement to actualize the demands of the Filipino people and also to place women on an equal footing with men in significant spheres of activity'. Liberating the Philippines from the domination of foreign economic powers presupposes reassessing the position of women in Philippine society; hence

> GABRIELA aims to educate, organize and mobilize women towards the elimination of all forms of oppression against women. . . and consolidate the organized strength of women for political action.[81]

In this context, the workers' struggle for improving their conditions in the world market factories of TNCs is viewed as part of a wider struggle for the creation of a society where people's needs are of paramount importance. In such a society, priority will be given, for example, to the elimination of 'child abuse, child prostitution, the varying degrees of exploitation in the form of child labour', that go hand in hand with the present economic crisis. Again, in connection with this goal of concentrating on real needs, 'women will stop at nothing to prevent [dangerous and irrelevant ventures such as] the Bataan Nuclear Plant from ever becoming operational'. This is because the only beneficiaries in these dangerous and costly projects would be the multinational corporation surrounding the area, the foreign countries from which the technology and raw materials will be imported, and a few individuals whose greed for profit can only be matched by their lack of interest in the people's welfare.[82]

The GABRIELA movement is gathering momentum in the Philippines and is providing a powerful forum for demanding an alternative path of development. Whether the principles of the movement will be replicated in other countries is difficult to predict. Each developing country is rooted in its own social, economic and often racial conflicts, which are bound to be reflected in the workers' struggles. Nonetheless, GABRIELA may provide a concrete model for women workers in other countries to emulate.

3. The capital comes home

The Third World in the midst of the First

While women in the South question the desirability of an externally controlled path of development, a new restructuring of industries gets under way in the advanced capitalist economies of the North. It is ironic that the pattern of this restructuring is showing itself to be very similar to that seen in many Third World countries in the last two decades; and once more, as in the Third World, the pattern involves a vital role for women.

Given the rapid changes in technology and market demand in many industries, it can be easier and more cost-effective for large corporations to have production facilities in areas which are not too distant from the centres of consumption and final use. This is especially so now that a sufficient reserve of cheap labour among the unemployed of the West can assure an effective check on potential wage increases. This explains, to some extent, why both in clothing and electronics there have been moves in recent years to locate production in First World countries. The tariff barrier, especially around the EEC, also induces large multinationals to produce in Europe for the European market in order to receive exemption from customs restrictions.

A combination of such factors has led to novel situations, where some multinational companies with homes in the Third World have located their sites in Europe. A growing group of multinationals from the newly industrializing countries (NICs) has been engaged for some time in locating production in other and poorer non-European countries. The EPZ areas of Sri Lanka and Bangladesh are favourite investment spots for TNCs from Hong Kong and the Philippines. Apart from the attraction of even lower labour costs than at home, these countries offer the multinationals of NICs the golden opportunity of 'tariff-hopping'. By locating in Bangladesh and Sri Lanka, the more successful companies in Hong Kong or the Philippines can, for example, circumvent the quotas imposed on their exports to the West by the Multifibre Agreement. However, some companies find that it can be even more profitable to source their production in the declining peripheral regions of Europe, as these allow the possibility of an open market in the EEC, and in some cases in the United States as well. There are additional advantages in being near the market: a rapid turnaround time and quick response to changes in demand. Moreover, regional grants offered to companies in the peripheral regions of Europe often subsidize the shift from areas of exceptionally low labour costs in the Third World to ones with relatively high costs in the First. The opening of a production site in Ireland by the Hong Kong-based Bonaventure Textiles Ltd in 1983 is an example of such a trend.[1]

The host regions in Europe have been particularly active in making it attractive for the TNCs to locate and to invest, with the help of the national governments. The legal and institutional frameworks that protect labour have been the major target in the process. Interference with the market mechanism is often claimed to be the major obstacle to job creation. In the spirit of the free market mechanism, therefore, Western governments, since the mid-1970s, have looked for an alternative economic structure that is likely to provide capital with sufficient freedom to grow. The powers of the nation-states have also been directed towards curbing the strength of the unions that may stand in the way of such expansions.

One such attempt to eliminate the fetter on profit-making and growth has been to devise institutions in the North similar to the Export Processing Zones. Enterprise Zones, as planned by the monetarist governments in Europe and the United States, are steps in this direction. A whole range of incentives, including exemption from rates and property taxes, are being offered to attract private investment and create employment. The zones have been viewed as an ideal substitute for public investment in the decaying inner-city areas. In the UK, there are now 28 Enterprise Zones, and six freeports. The impact of these zones on jobs has been doubtful; it seems as if only the property speculators have benefited. The commercial areas located near the zones have become wastelands, as firms 'boundary hop' to take advantage of the incentive.

In the United States, the Reagan administration has been planning to set up a number of zones across the country, encouraging states to be as flexible and innovative as possible in reducing the constraints on capital. The original proposal was to modify the minimum wages as an inducement to locate in an Enterprise Zone. Although this inducement was withdrawn after trade union opposition, the zones still offer considerable freedom from health, safety and environmental regulations.[2]

The Enterprise Zones are not primarily designed for tax-free export production, but it is possible to develop export-processing industries in such zones. The Belgian government has plans to create employment zones ('zones d'emploi') in regions with high unemployment, with many of the features of Export Processing Zones. In Britain, the design to create freeports is being launched as a logical extension of the liberalization and deregulation programmes of a monetarist government.[3] In such plans, the advanced countries of the West are now looking towards the success-stories of the South in search of a model to emulate.

There is a wry twist to this role-reversal between North and South. The Adam Smith Institute, a think-tank for monetarist policies, passionately urges Britain to learn from the Far Eastern experience:

> . . . although there are not Freeports in the United Kingdom, the development of Hong Kong under British rule has been a spectacular testament to the sucess of Freeport policy. Taiwan and Singapore have enjoyed similar success with Freeports, with South Korea and Malaysia numbered among those seeking to partake of the growth which the freeport concept achieved there. More recent examples from the Philippines and Sri Lanka seem set to achieve the same.

In order to achieve similar degrees of success, certain concessions, of course, would have to be offered:

> Tax relief on investment . . . exemption from planning per-

mission and restrictions and more controversially, exemptions from certain national regulations, such as the current 'protection of employment' rules. The Protection of Employment Act is a considerable inhibitor on new firms starting up in business, and it would be instructive to look at the effects of giving certain concessions within the Freeports; the same can be said of the operation of minimum wage rules.[4]

A textiles firm director told the *Financial Times* optimistically: 'I have this vision that St Helens could become the Hong Kong of the North West.'[5]

Section I: THE ELECTRONICS INDUSTRY IN BRITAIN AND IRELAND

Development agencies and multinational investment

While the possibilities of introducing institutions similar to Export Processing Zones are thus being debated in the West, foreign investments are being enticed into the depressed regions through other means. Scotland, South Wales and Ireland have been particularly successful in their attempts to attract foreign investment, as they offer, apart from attractive tax-reliefs and investment grants, a supply of cheap and English-speaking labour – a quality Japanese and American multinationals particularly value. Regional Development Agencies in Scotland and Wales have been especially welcoming to high-tech industries with growth potential, in order to counteract the devastating effects that declining industries such as coal, steel and shipbuilding have had on the majority of the working population in these regions. Similarly, the Irish Development Agency has looked to foreign investment in high-tech industries to offset the massive de-industrialization and consequent unemployment in the traditional manufacturing sector.

The electronics industry has been particularly popular with development agencies, since it has become virtually synonymous with rapid and far-reaching technical innovations. The potential of the ubiquitous silicon chip is widely advertised, and planners see in the industry a foundation for a dramatic and thoroughgoing social transformation, often termed the second (or third, or fourth) industrial revolution. Government spokesmen and the media project an image of future development whereby the depressed regions of Wales, Scotland and Ireland could one day achieve the same dynamism as that of Silicon Valley in California, where innovations in semiconductor technology began and grew at an exponential rate. Silicon Glen – a publicity term to conjure up this futurist image of Scotland – is typical of the projected dream. Foreign investments are supposed to create that 'critical mass' – a metaphor to denote a particular density of investment which, once achieved, would automatically lead to the self-sustained growth of an indigenous electronics industry.

In fact, the promise of such a decisive leap to self-sustained growth is unlikely to be realized. Investments by American and Japanese multinationals in the peripheral regions of mature economies in Europe are mainly of a 'branch plant' type. Here the foreign-owned plants are merely an intermediary stage in an international division of labour organized within the transnational corporations. Documentations by Peter Murray and James Wickham reveal, for example, that

> Foreign-owned enterprises generally process and assemble raw materials imported to Ireland, usually from an affiliate of the parent company, and then export the product, usually again to an affiliate of the same company.[1]

The scope of technology-transfer in such a situation is really rather small. The hope of having greater control over the industry also seems distant. The Scottish Education and Action for Development (SEAD) report, *Electronics and Development*, highlights the problem:

> Even if Scotland's research effort is growing, the degree of external control of the Scottish industry means that there is no guarantee that the end product of the research and development process will be manufactured in Scotland.[2]

The Welsh situation is remarkably similar. Kevin Morgan and Andrew Sayer in their report *The International Electronics Industry and Regional Development in Britain* observe:

> While every regional and local development authority hopes that this 'seed-bed' effect will happen in its own area, in the very nature of the industry it cannot happen in more than a few simultaneously, simply because there are not enough front-end production and R & D [Research and Development] opportunities to go round. We think it most unlikely that South Wales could achieve even Scotland's modest success.[3]

Indeed the backward linkage with the domestic economy in these regions, as in the Third World, is very small. Given the structure of industry and market opportunities, the Scottish Development Agency (SDA) consultants Booz, Allen and Hamilton concluded as early as 1978 that the scope of Scottish-owned companies, apart from subcontracting and component supply, lay only in the industrial and commercial application of electronics.

The technological base of the semiconductor industry in these regions is qualitatively rather different from that in the export platforms of Third World countries. Whereas the latter were explored mainly for repetitive, unskilled assembly and testing work, the regional peripheries in the UK and Europe are used for wafer fabrication as well. Although South Wales and Ireland still specialize mainly in the assembling and testing side of the industry, Scotland's transition, since the mid-1970s, to the more capital-intensive and technologically demanding work of wafer fabrication has been quite impressive. According to the SDA, Scotland has the highest concentration of wafer fabrication for computer chips in Europe. The region now boasts of 80 per cent of UK microchip production and more than 20 per cent of European capacity. Six large multinational companies – National Semiconductor, NEC (formerly Nippon Electric), Motorola, Hughes, Burr-Brown and General Instruments – have wafer fabrication plants in Scotland. More foreign investments in this area are to follow. The close proximity of sources of raw materials such as silicon and pure gases have added strength to Scotland's microchip industry. It is with some pride that the SDA pronounces that Scotland manufactures more microchips per head than any other region in the world and that the annual turn-over of Scottish-based facilities is more than £350 million.[4]

But behind the publicity blitz there remains a nagging doubt as to whether this one-stage transition to the 'front-end' of production really connotes any technological lead. Although designing the wafers involves substantial capital inputs, the production does not require much skilled work. It is still the semi-skilled and unskilled operators who tend to perform the routine loading, unloading, cleaning, monitoring and processing tasks in wafer fabrication. In an industry where technology is highly 'encapsulated' in the product, upgrading the technological status of the operation does not necessarily mean upgrading the technological skill.[5]

The scope of technology transfer recedes even further with the third phase of development, where the application of automation in the assembly stage of production reduces the importance of direct labour in the final stages. The effect of automation on the assembly line is generally to reduce the remaining assembly-line workers to the status of mere 'machine minders'.

In fact, as the new pattern of investment in the British Isles indicates, the attractions of Third World locations are generally fading. As the wage levels in some of the newly industrializing countries increase and the women workers there become more assertive, it makes sense for the large companies to transfer production to peripheral European regions, such as Scotland, which can offer attractive financial incentives and an adequate infra-structure. It is not just a coincidence, therefore, that when the Japanese company NEC announced plans to invest in a £40 million facility in Livingston New Town in 1980 it was for a joint assembly and wafer fabrication plant. However, the assembly facility was scheduled to come into operation two years ahead of the fabrication facility. At present Motorola, which has one of its biggest fabrication plants at East Kilbride, sends semiconductor products for assembly to offshore plants in the Far East. The same plant, however, is currently investing £60 million to create integrated production facilities at East

Kilbride, which will have its own automated testing and assembly capacity.[6]

The return of international capital to peripheral regions of Europe has had, for understandable reasons, very little spin-off effect. In Scotland, Scottish-owned companies contribute only 16 per cent of the total electronic employment. In Ireland, Irish firms account for 31 per cent of the electronic employment, but this is confined to very small firms employing less than 25 people and with limited Research and Development. In South Wales, foreign multinationals such as Matshushita, Mitel and Siliconix dominate the electronics industry and account for almost all of the employment in advanced electronics production.

The development of the electronics industry, therefore, to quote Morgan and Sayer, indicates development *in* the region rather than *of* the region.[7] This pattern of development has been dictated by technological advances and the consequent need of international capital to restructure internationally. The electronics industry, especially the semiconductor side of it, has always been subject to rapidly increasing economies of scale, which on average lower the price by 25 per cent a year. Coupled with the fact that the cost of entry, especially for R & D, is rising all the time, the falling price of chips makes the cash-flow problem acute in this industry. It is not only that the economies of scale lower the price of chips, but also that the technological advances increase the power of each chip, with the result that a given level of demand can be met by fewer of them. This explains why competition is so fierce and over-production so common in an industry where the market is growing so rapidly.

Being ahead of the rest in this scenario pays enormous dividends. Because the potential profit through being a year ahead in this technological race is so large, the companies are compelled to spend huge amounts on R & D. However, they welcome subsidization of labour-intensive parts of production through regional grants or tax incentives, such as are offered by the competing development agencies in Western Europe or by the nation-states of the Third World.

The 'new wave' of American and Japanese electronics investments has shown a perceptible shift of preference from the Export Processing Zones of developing countries to English-speaking peripheral regions in Europe. The reasons are manifold. Besides the significant advantages already mentioned in carrying out the final stages of assembly behind EEC tariff barriers, especially in the case of products destined for European markets, there is the possibility of government grants towards research. The university network, as in Scotland, effectively subsidizes the cost of training technical personnel. It also finances minor R & D that is geared to an adaptation of American and Japanese products to European market conditions. The genuinely high-skill aspects of the labour process, however, remain in the US and Japan.

In spite of the high-tech, dynamic image of the industry that is being projected by the Welsh, Irish and Scottish Development Agencies, the nature of investment in these regions bears close resemblance to that of investment in the offshore plants of newly industrializing countries. The cynical comment of Murray and Wickham summarizes the state of affairs very precisely:

> While European development agencies tend to claim that they have 'chosen' electronics as a growth area, the reality is the other way round. The electronics industry's ability to relocate its production processes internationally and its desperate need for extra sources of finance have ensured that in fact *it* has chosen *them*. The success or otherwise of the different and competing agencies is only a factor *within* the general situation. However . . . the electronics industry is being presented not just as creating jobs, but as being an industry that is uniquely suited to national needs. Such statements illustrate . . . [the agencies'] promotional flair rather than [their] grasp of reality.[8]

Gender and the changing structure of employment

The single most important contribution of electronics TNCs in the depressed regions of the UK and the Irish Republic has been in the creation of new jobs. The significance of this contribution, however, lies less in the number of jobs, which has not been remarkable, than in the creation of a new type of working class, totally different from the traditional militant unionized labour force of the industrial zones of yesteryear. In the process, TNCs have transferred to the British Isles a new brand of management practices and a new model of unionism, that may change fundamentally the nature of the labour movement as we know it today.

Over the last 10 years, Scotland has lost over 200,000 manufacturing and mining jobs. With the decimation of steel, shipbuilding and mining, the level of unemployment among male workers in industrial zones such as West Lothian today exceeds 40 per cent.[9] With a predicted average loss of 30,000 jobs in the Scottish manufacturing sector alone each year, the worst effects are yet to come. As against this, the electronics industry has to date created only 43,000 jobs in Scotland all told. The cost per job has been as high as £20,000 to £40,000 in terms of regional subsidies.[10] In spite of such heavy subsidization, the total number

of jobs in this industry, which has never been high, is unlikely to go up very much in future. In the early 1970s, employment in the industry did grow reasonably and the level of employment – around 50,000 – was higher than it is today. Employment rose as the electronic processes replaced electro-mechanical production, but dropped drastically with the recession between 1974 and 1980. The industry has picked up again since then, but the level of employment has yet to return to the peak achieved in the early 1970s.

The limited success of the industry in creating new jobs is particularly significant in Scotland, where the electronics industry has a reasonably long history. During the Second World War, the Manchester-based firm Ferranti, specializing in defence electronics, transferred some of their operations to Edinburgh. The base of the industry thereafter was replenished by the advent of some well-known American companies, such as Borrough, Honeywell and NCR, producing office and business machinery. By 1950, with the entry of IBM, Scotland had already become a favourite place of investment by foreign electronics TNCs. The philosophy 'What is good for IBM is good for us' attracted a number of other well-known electronics companies. The move into Scotland was further expedited when, in the late 1960s, some famous US names in the semiconductor industry, such as Motorola and National Semiconductor, established plants in Scotland for assembly work. By the 1970s, the region was already moving towards wafer fabrication on a massive scale. In spite of this impressive record of the development of the industry in the region, the effect on jobs has been very modest.

In South Wales the foreign firms arrived only from 1974, and the level of employment in electronics grew only marginally between 1974 and 1981. The highest level of employment ever achieved in this industry was around 30,000, before the deepening of the recession in 1979, and this figure is unlikely to be exceeded in the future. In the Irish Republic, the total number of jobs created in the electronics industry so far is around 11,000, and again the number is not predicted to rise any further.[11] The response of leading electronics companies to interviews taken by Morgan and Sayer is revealing in this context:

All the firms were asked what would be the employment effects of a significant increase in output – say of 20 per cent. In all but one case, the answer was either zero or a very small increase.[12]

This trend towards stagnation in employment is partly due to increased automation on the factory floor and partly to a marked intensification of labour, through longer production runs and the reducing of set-up time and other 'dead' time. Although the use of automation in the assembly line has, to a certain extent, shifted the locational advantage to the North, the South may still attract considerable investment by offering workforces that are poorly paid and willing to work more flexibly and intensively, thereby allowing companies to maximize the return on investment costs of the new automated processes. Hugh Smearton, chairman and founder of the successful electronics firm Fortronic, put the Scottish workers in perspective. He warned that big investment would be necessary if Scotland was to remain competitive with the Far East in assembly work: 'The only way we can make such investment pay is to run it round the clock. We can't do it on a 38-hour week.'[13]

A flexible workforce which is willing to work at a greater speed when necessary is an important requirement for a TNC when it invests in these peripheral regions. Since to American and Japanese TNCs such investments represent only offshore locations, such regions understandably are among the first to suffer from cuts during the slumps that occur periodically in the electronics market. In this volatile market, hiring a large number of permanent workers during a boom period can prove risky, because getting rid of them can be costly and troublesome.

The viability of the electronics industry in these peripheral regions, therefore, requires a cheap, flexible and disposable workforce. This means a new proletariat, which is outside the tradition of the highly unionized coal and steel industries, that have earned Scotland and South Wales the reputation of being the most radical regions in the British Isles. Such a preferred labour force was provided by the daughters and wives of the ex-steelworkers and ex-miners. Incoming firms tend to favour young workers with little previous experience, and hence little to unlearn, so that they can adjust to the new forms of work and social organization. As the SEAD report comments:

> The electronics companies have never sought their labour among redundant shipyard workers and coalminers. Their requirement for a manually dexterous and pliant workforce willing to accept long hours of repetitive work was most likely to be met by female workers with limited experience of manufacturing and of trade unions than by the craft skilled and militant workforce bred by Scotland's traditional industries.[14]

Indeed, the feminization of the industry, where nearly 50 per cent of the workforce and the majority of production line workers are women, is the most significant effect of the expansion of the electronics industry in Scotland, South Wales and Ireland. It has radically changed the gender structure of employment, especially among semi-skilled and non-craft workers (Table 5).

Table 5: A typical example of European peripheral regions: gender composition of electronics workforce in Ireland in 1981

Occupation Group	Employee	Per cent	Females	Per cent Female in each group
Managers	725	6.4	32	4.4
Supervisors	581	5.1	141	24.3
Administrative	444	3.9	143	32.2
Professional	607	5.3	45	7.4
Technicians	886	7.8	33	3.7
Clerical	848	7.5	609	71.8
Craftsmen	348	3.1	4	1.2
Non-craft production workers	6,527	57.4	4,695	71.9
Others	372	3.2	93	25.0
Total	11,338		5,795	(51.1)

Source: Graham Day (ed), Diversity and Decomposition In The Labour Market, UK: Gower, 1982, p. 186.

The direction of technological changes in the last few years has altered the structure of employment in these regions in yet another way. Traditional electro-mechanical skills are increasingly being replaced by more specialized skills or by multi-skilled technicians who can switch between jobs. The chasm between the work of semi-skilled, largely female operatives and that of emerging multi-skilled technicians or graduate engineers has entailed the elimination of the middle rank of blue-collar workers – the traditional mainstay of radical unionization. The new industrialization policy has in effect undermined the male-dominated working class of the British Isles.

The expanding electronics industry has done very little to alleviate the acute rise in male unemployment among the working class in these regions. In the growing West Lothian electronics industry, the director of the new Bathgate Area Support Enterprise (BASE) sees very little prospect for the 2,000 male workers who were made redundant at the Leyland Truck plant in 1984. 'That kind of employment goes to 17-year-old girls or technologists or graduates.'[15]

The reasons behind the feminization of the industry

The reasons for preferring women to men workers are broadly similar to those that prevail in Third World countries. 'Nimble fingers', 'natural dexterity', 'patience', are the attributes ascribed to women workers when they are recruited for unskilled and repetitive work. There is an irony in the stereotyping itself, as the recruitment on these grounds implies certain social skills which men generally lack. In the job market, however, skill is often defined in an ideologically biased way, to construct a hierarchical distinction between the sexes. Male workers are pushed to acquire skilled status not just to get higher pay but in order to attain a status that becomes identified with masculinity and with the claims of the breadwinner. In light assembly work in general and in the electronics industry in particular, women are employed for their 'natural manual dexterity'. This dexterity, however, as I have discussed before, is not 'natural' at all, but the result of informal training in domestic labour which, because it occurs in the home, does not appear in official definitions. Such processes nonetheless ensure that in the electronics industry, as elsewhere, 'skill has been increasingly defined against women – skilled work is work that women do not do'.[16]

The ideologically constructed definition of skill, however, can be used effectively by management to introduce a new social organization in the business world. To start with, women workers, when defined as unskilled or semi-skilled, can be paid far less than the average wage of male employees in the manufacturing sector. Even from the extremely patchy data that are available, it appears that the basic rates of pay for semi-skilled women workers in the electronics industry are about half those of miners and steelworkers. In 1983 the basic rates of pay for semi-skilled workers in the industry were, on average, £77 to £88 per week excluding bonuses. The average weekly earning of a miner in

Britain in the same year, according to the New Earnings Survey, was £183.26 per week, and that of a steelworker £165.20 per week.[17] The implications of such low wages for female workers had a significant effect on the levels of poverty. Most of the women were wives and daughters of redundant male workers, and hence were the major if not sole breadwinners of their families. Their incomes must be assessed against the findings of the Royal Commission on the Distribution of Income and Wealth in 1980 that considered workers receiving less than £85.50 per week to be low paid.[18] But women are not perceived as major breadwinners, and may even be expected to 'feel grateful for not being on an assembly line packing poultry in Chunky Chicken factory'.[19] At all events the new jobs hardly bring new levels of affluence to the stricken regions.

As in the Third World, women workers are 'ghettoized' in assembly line work, with poor prospects of promotion. The most that a woman worker can hope for is promotion to the post of quality controller or line supervisor. Women, therefore, provide the broad base of an occupational pyramid which becomes more male-dominated as it rises to its peak. The new type of proletariat is definitely congenial to the management. As the manager of Nikita (UK) reported: 'Whilst not being anti-union, we are a non-union plant; there is a tendency for women to be less interested in unions than men.'[20] The limited involvement of women with the trade union movement in these areas that have been bastions of a radical working class is the result of the historical exclusion of women from craft-based work. As E. Breitenbach has shown, Scottish women's lower wages have long roots in history.[21] When the factory system was initially introduced in the early nineteenth century it was common to find the family division of labour transplanted into the factory. The father fulfilled a supervisory role in relation to women and children working with him. This hierarchical division of labour was also associated with differential rates of pay. It was assumed that women should receive lower rates of pay, and so men excluded women from certain jobs in order to protect their own higher rates. Over the years, Scottish women were not only excluded from certain jobs but also systematically debarred from union organization.

This is because, between 1850 and 1880, protection of sectional interests – those of crafts and skilled trades – became the basis of union organization. Women, being already excluded from crafts and skilled trades which were dominated by men, had very little scope to acquire political power in such a system.

In these respects, however, the history of the development of Scottish trade unionism is not so very different from that in the rest of Britain. Because of assumptions that have their roots in pre-capitalist and patriarchal society, women were generally excluded from union organizations. To be able to gain access to working-class political organizations, workers had to have acquired craft skills; however, it was men who regulated entry into skilled trades as well as the acquisition of certain skills. In the printing industry, for example, the male compositors militantly excluded women from the composing room; and by doing so,

---

Women in unions: the experience of Scotland

Elsie: . . . when I went down to Eastbourne . . . to conferences and that, it was all males, the majority of places [i.e. unions] always send males . . . actually there was only two females at that conference for youths [secretaries] from all over, AUEW [sent] one [i.e. herself].

Sal: See, after office hours, men take over . . . women [are] not allowed to go for meetings; among the shop stewards . . . politics stops in the factory and isn't carried on at home, there – men take over . . . often women accept their husbands' [authority in the home] . . . and don't go for meetings after work

Annie: . . . makes me feel guilty for it [going to union meetings] . . . although he is perfectly capable to take care of the children . . . he can go off to meetings without much trouble.

Rosie: No problems for me . . . with my husband . . . *if* I cook the meals, he'll heat up the food but not cook it.

Elsie: Yeah, you have to get the house organized first.

Source: Interview with women workers of Transistor (UK), Scotland, by Yut-Lin Wong, *Ghettoization of Women Workers in the Electronics Industry*, IDS, Sussex University, 1983.

they also barred women in the printing industry from their powerful craft unions, the Typographical Association of England or
the Scottish Typographical Association.[22]

The patterns of sectionalism and male domination of trade unions caused Scotswomen to be relatively marginalized in the
trade union movement, notwithstanding their high participation
in the manufacturing labour force. In spite of this, Scottish
women have a long history of taking up the challenge of capital.
The seven-month occupation of Lee Jeans Company (a subsidiary of Vanity Fair Corporation) by 140 women workers in
1981, in protest against the closure of the factory in Greenock, is
a typical example of solidarity shown by Scottish women. The
position of female workers on the fringe of the trade union movement is not the result of the inherent docility of women workers
as such, but the historical consequence of the long gender
struggle within the union movement itself.

In South Wales, unlike Scotland, women were largely excluded from paid employment until recently. While women did
enter the labour force in increasing numbers after the Second
World War, following a growth in service and 'light' industries,
even in the mid-1960s the proportion of women working was as
low as 20 per cent in some towns. The reason could be the nature
and exclusiveness of male employment in the mining and steel
industries, and the role of women's domestic labour in servicing
the breadwinners.[23] The 'green' labour that the region offered,
therefore, itself reflected the unequal power-gender system
within the working class.[24] The politics of gender is likewise reflected in the male-centred behaviour of the unions. In their
survey of the electronics industry in South Wales, Morgan and
Sayer found that management and unions broadly concurred on
the female stereotype. One male union official said that he would
prefer to represent a thousand men rather than a dozen women.
This is because women are 'less rational'.[25]

New management practices

Recruitment of female workers, therefore, is a conscious
strategy to tap a source of 'green' labour, of workers who are not
steeped in the tradition of unionization. This altering gender-

structure of employment has also been associated with a changing location of production. If the legacy of the radical labourist culture persists in a locality, the companies seek alternative sites within the region. The new town of East Kilbride has become a popular location for inward investment in the electronics industry; significantly it is nine miles south of Glasgow, a traditional bastion of unionized labour. The other new towns, particularly Livingston and Glenrothes, similarly provided alternative 'greenfield sites'. In Wales too, managers were aware of the contrasts within South Wales – especially between the valley communities of the coalfield and the coastal belt to the south and east where many managers lived. The Welsh Development Agency (WDA) 'sold' this area to the big corporations in their frenetic attempts to eradicate Welsh industrial history. The WDA's recently established 'golden triangle' in Gwent is such an attempt. The triangle has not only the advantage of easy access to England, but has a labour force similar to that in the 'M4 corridor' labour market (along the London–Bristol axis: a favourite spot for indigenous innovatory electronics firms). It comprises more of a middle-class society who are already attuned to corporate mores and are less interested in unionization.[26]

The 'green' labour in the 'greenfield sites' has allowed foreign companies to introduce a new brand of management practices. This has also been facilitated by selective recruitment procedures. The age-group of female operators in the electronics industry is not as clustered as that in the Third World countries, where most electronics workers are single and aged between 16 and 25. In South Wales, Scotland and Ireland they are spread across a much wider range of ages. Some firms explicitly show preference for young school-leavers. The Japanese semiconductor firm, Nippon Electrical Company (NEC), for example, has a policy of recruiting female school-leavers for its Livingston factory. The average age of its workforce today is reported to be 21. However, in general, single women are employed alongside married women without children and married women with grown-up children. The single most important quality that is looked for in labour is its flexibility and compliance with the new tendencies in personnel management.

American electronic companies are well known for their anti-pathy towards unions. A report in 1984 showed that in Scotland up to 44 per cent of US-owned plants of all sizes in all industries were not unionized. The proportion is much higher among elec-tronics firms, where nearly 63 per cent of American firms do not recognize unions.[27] The most effective way to forestall unioniza-tion in these firms is to introduce a direct and regular form of communication between the workers and the management, even with respect to routine grievances traditionally taken up by shop-stewards. Such a personal 'listening' system undermines class solidarity and defuses potential militancy among factory workers. In the words of a woman cited by Yut-Lin Wong:

> . . . every so often . . . you go and have an informal lunch with him [the Managing Director] and he talks to you about the place and tells you about himself and everything . . . you can ask him anything you like, it was really good![28]

As a part of this personalized management practices package, 'quality circles' or 'involvement teams' are introduced on the shop floor. The idea of quality circles, strictly speaking, is to en-hance the quality of output by utilizing the knowledge and skill of the workforce. But the major advantage to the corporations is that they encourage workers to develop a management perspec-tive on work – to think about how costs can be cut and produc-tivity improved, even if this ultimately means redundancies for workers. Quality circle meetings also allow supervisors to iden-tify pro-management employees and pick up useful information about what is going on on the shop floor. To a worker the circles are likely to give a sense of belonging, a sense of having a part in the management process, but in practice circles often lead to a fragmentation of the workforce, with circle members seen as fav-oured in the eyes of the rest of the employees. Also, different quality circles in a company see themselves as competitors. It is not surprising that, in Britain, management consultants have rec-ommended quality circles to the British companies as an effec-tive way of undermining union power.[29]

A number of US firms, following the IBM model, project an image of 'benevolent' employers, claiming that unionization is not necessary. Siliconix, a US semiconductor firm in South Wales, asserts that, since wages and conditions are above average, and management is open and accessible, unionization is not necessary. The company has operated in South Wales since 1974 without any industrial relations problem and without any demand for union recognition from the shop floor. American companies in general are aggressive in their anti-unionism and often counteract potential demands for unionization through shareholdings and profit-sharing among workers; they view 'unionization [as] . . . an unnecessary artificial barrier between management and workforce'.[30]

An essential part of this new type of personnel management is to reduce the hierarchical division of labour within the factory by eliminating some of the middle tiers of workers, particularly foremen and supervisors. Apart from increasing the output per worker, this system enables management to have greater access to the shop floor and to pave the way for a new type of negotiation.

New brands of unionism

Unlike American firms, Japanese companies have generally welcomed unionization on the shop floor, and the level of unionization not only in Japanese firms but even (notwithstanding the example of Siliconix) in American ones in regions like South Wales has been quite high. The managers' perception of unions in these firms has also been favourable. Managers view unions as means towards an 'ordered environment' and discipline, rather than as agents of trouble and dispute. This is also true of firms that have allowed unions in Scotland. From a survey taken by the Scottish Development Agency of US electronics firms in Scotland in 1981,

> One of the most impressive results to emerge was the large percentage (92 per cent) of unionized plants who considered that unions either had a favourable or neutral impact on plant operations. From a management perspective, there is a strong indication of the sound industrial relations based on cooperation which US plants have successfully nurtured in a unionized environment.[31]

'Co-operation rather than conflict' is the new spirit of Japanese-style unionism that is now being introduced into the British Isles with the entry of the foreign multinationals. It is being acclimatized with the help of some specific deals. First, it has been customary to adhere to 'single unionism'. While all unions may legitimately seek to recruit, once agreement has been reached between a company and a union, all others are obliged to withdraw. By eliminating or squeezing the status-hierarchy among production workers, it has been possible to obliterate one of the major *raisons d'être* of multi-unionism. Single unionism inevitably leads to competition between unions to recruit members among electronics workers. This again leads to concessions of principle to management by the unions concerned, in order to win an agreement with a company. 'Sweetheart deals', whereby workers are simply assigned to a union before a factory has even been opened, are one of the concessions that a company can stipulate in the new climate of unionism. The chosen union, in this case, becomes an institution imposed on the workers by the company and pre-empts any rank-and-file organizations.

The most successful British union to have agreements with American and Japanese electronics companies is the Electrical, Electronics Telecommunication and Plumbing Trade Union, (EETPU). This union is proud of its new strategies and of its success with the TNCs:

> . . . the traditional approach is not enough. What these companies want is a union that will do its utmost to avoid strikes and that is what we offer them. We give co-operation rather than confrontation.[32]

The EETPU already has a number of 'no-strike' agreements with electronic companies. The first of these was signed in 1981 with Toshiba at its plant in Plymouth. The agreement includes an acceptance of 'pendulum' arbitration, where power of arbitration is given to an external third party. The EETPU has similarly concluded an agreement with the Japanese company Sanyo in Lowestoft, where production in the plant is run in the style of a Japanese management regime:

This includes meticulous inspection of productivity and quality details, no smoking, talking, eating or listening to music on the production line. Workers have to wait with a hand up until a supervisor allows a toilet break.[33]

As a spokesman from the Association of Scientific, Technical and Managerial Staff (ASTMS) says: 'If what the EETPU are currently offering multinational companies in the UK was implemented in a Third World country, the British TUC would make a complaint to the ILO.'[34]

Workers' resistance to this new brand of unionism is reduced by yet another emerging organizational innovation, whereby the workforce is divided between 'core' and 'peripheral' workers. The distinction is based not simply on technical skill or job-content but

> good company employees are seen in terms of attendance, adaptability, responsibility, discipline, identification with the company and above all work-rate and quality. The use of this concept of skill is perhaps most common in Japanese plants. In one of these, some newly arrived Japanese managers mistook the traditional British categories of skilled, unskilled and semi-skilled as meaning good, bad or indifferent . . . to company favoured practices.[35]

Once classified, the companies try their best to insulate the core workers from the fluctuations of a volatile market. One firm coined the term 'rings of defence' to denote the peripheral workers, who are hired on fixed-term contracts to meet the production quota during the upturn of the market. Subcontracting is also used to provide a cheap way of meeting the employment needs of the company during boom periods. Achieving flexibility in labour-recruitment in this way is a step on the way to the Japanese practice of offering 'jobs for life' to a core group of workers by utilizing the casual labour of part-time and temporary workers, as well as that of subcontractors. However divisive this policy may be, it has been effective in persuading the unions to accept the foreign control with remarkable alacrity. The promise of more secure employment with the transnational companies has led the shop-stewards, in the case of an Anglo–Japanese joint venture, to invite the headquarters in Tokyo to assume full control of the company union![36]

These new brands of unionism are significant with regard to the changing nature of employment for women in the industry. With increased automation and recession, there has been a trend towards 'defeminization of the industry'. The possibility of a growing demand for custom chips (known as Application Specific Chips) in place of mass-produced 'jelly-bean' chips may reduce the demand for a permanent female workforce on the assembly line even further. Also, the skills that the electronics industry expect of its assembly-line workers are in the process of change. With the onset of automated wafer fabrication, Nance Goldstein observed in 1983 that women operators in Scotland are becoming merely 'machine minders, monitoring the movement of wafer batches through highly complex equipment, reading the computerized performance data output and sounding the alarm if something goes wrong'.[37]

The change in the desired skills is not going to stop here. The electronics industry, like many other manufacturing industries, is now poised to adopt a fully integrated computer-controlled system. This system contrasts with the partial and piecemeal computerized automation adopted so far. In managerial terminology, the 'islands of automation' are now to be replaced by an 'integrated system' where *one* central computer controls all the machine tools, work stations and the transference of components and tooling. Besides the potential overall control that the system offers to management, it has the unique advantage of producing a wide range of goods in small numbers. A small change in programming will ensure custom-made products at very little extra cost. For those who can afford to spend a few million pounds at 1986 prices, the economies of scale are now being superseded by the economies of variety, with the help of the 'Flexible Manufacturing System' (FMS).

The implications of FMS for the structure of employment deserve careful consideration. The robots are not likely to replace human labour entirely, but the need for direct operatives will be drastically reduced. In contrast, there will be a need for a new type of core workers who are 'functionally flexible'. As *Works Management*, November 1985, states:

> The age of the individual craftsman is passing, to be replaced by a new breed of multiskilled workers able to look after complex integrated systems which might involve anything from hydraulics through electronics, electrics and pneumatics.[38]

In order to make the investment worthwhile, the companies will have to ensure full and constant utilization of automated plants. For this, 'Jacks of all trade' who are expert in fault-finding and maintenance will be essential. In other words, there will be greater demand for technical and engineering skills rather than for the types of skill women are traditionally taught at home, which give them dexterity in assembly-line jobs.

In Britain as a whole, the industry has already seen dramatic job losses among female workers in recent years. Between 1971 and 1981, over 90 per cent of total job losses in electronics have been among female workers. The same period has seen a growth in the recruitment of multi-skilled engineers or technicians, who are predominantly male (see Figure 3, p.104). It is easier for males to achieve the quality of 'multi-skill good company employees'. Hence it is the male workers who are likely to be termed 'core' employees, with all the guaranteed employment contracts the term entails. Women will then conveniently fill the role of peripheral workers, who would be hired and fired in response to changed demand. In fact the much-publicized Japanese system of 'lifetime employment' scarcely applies to women, who account for 57 per cent of all factory workers in Japan. There, women factory workers are expected to leave their job in their early twenties and get married, rejoining the labour market, if at all, as part-timers only. In most cases neither temporary workers, part-timers nor women workers are represented by the unions in Japan.

The coming home of capital, therefore, has been accompanied by deep-rooted changes in work practices that are destined to alter the very nature of the working class. The initial feminization of the electronics industry, accompanied by a gradual reduc-

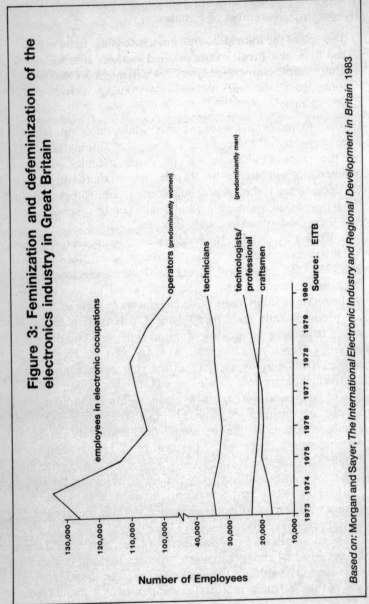

Figure 3: Feminization and defeminization of the electronics industry in Great Britain

Based on: Morgan and Sayer, *The International Electronic Industry and Regional Development in Britain* 1983

tion or casualization of direct labour, may indeed reduce the trade union movement in this sector to a mere sectional interest-group, representing an elite of technical and predominantly male workers. This experience is not going to be unique, either to the electronics industry as a sector or to the UK as a country. Technological changes and new management practices are creating increased polarization of the labour market in all sectors of the economy, in virtually all industrialized countries.

Section II: FLEXIBLE MANNING AND WOMEN OUTWORKERS

Flexible specialization and duality in the labour force

The concepts of core and periphery are no longer used simply to describe the differentiation between the metropolis and the ex-colonies, but also to describe an emerging dichotomy between the core (elite) workers and the peripheral (casual) workers within a national boundary.[1] In this new division, as in the case of the global division of labour, race and gender provide the most effective grounds for the stratification devised by the corporate managers. The changing style of personnel management in large companies – well exemplified, as we have seen, in the electronics industry in Scotland and Wales – is one of the factors contributing to this emergent dualism in the labour force. A second contributory factor is the use of subcontracting by large companies and a concomitant increase in the small business sector.

After years of decline, the small business sector has really made a comeback in the West in the last 10 years. Since the definition of small business varies from one country to another, it is difficult to make accurate inter-country comparisons of its rise. However, the published statistics point to definite and far-reaching shifts in its favour in almost all the mature capitalist countries in the world. In America, in spite of a rise in total sales, *Fortune*'s 500 companies – America's top industrial corporations –

reduced their total employment by 10 per cent between 1974 and 1984. In their place smaller companies who employ fewer than 500 people have increased their intakes by a phenomenal 2.7 million.[2] In the UK, the share of small firms – employing fewer than 100 people – in manufacturing employment has increased from 15 per cent in 1973 to 20 per cent in 1980. The trend has accelerated since then.[3] The pattern of growth is similar in other OECD countries and is particularly spectacular in Italy, where minifirms employing fewer than 20 people account for at least one-third of the total industrial workforce. An expansion of 345,000 jobs in Italian minifirms between 1971 and 1978 stands in sharp contrast to the massive shedding of labour, well above half a million, in the large manufacturing corporations.[4]

A rise in the small firms sector has gone hand-in-hand with a rise in the number of self-employed people. In the US, the number of self-employed increased by 30 per cent from 1970 to 1983, representing a rise of 2.1 million people. In Britain, there was an increase of about 300,000 self-employed from the early 1970s to 1983.

The growing importance of self-employment and of the small business sector indicates a pronounced change in the structure of business organizations. To some, it seems a welcome trend, indicating a reversal of the domination of large corporations. The phenomenon of small businesses often evokes a strong image of self-sufficient, individualistic economic units that have 'growing concern with the quality of life . . . under the slogan "small is beautiful" '.[5] A recent article by Graham Bannock projects the idealistic image of a future centred on small units of production:

> We may yet see a return to a brewery and a bakery in every small community, and certainly telematics and micro-processors will allow more and more people to work at home in what Alvin Toffler calls the 'electronic cottage'.[6]

However attractive this future vision may be, the present growth of small units of production is only marginally the result of the flowering of small entrepreneurship. It arises primarily out of the strategy of large corporations for 'putting out' as much work as is technologically and organizationally possible. In some industries, especially in clothing and electronics, international subcontracting has been seen as one way of surviving the oligopolistic competition. But another, perhaps more effective method of counteracting the falling level of profits has been to decentralize production, taking it to smaller units. These units are hardly independent: for most products, the retail outlet is controlled chiefly by a handful of large retailers. The small business sector in this scenario therefore becomes simply the equivalent of 'outside factories' for large corporate organizations. The method of decentralizing production through massive subcontracting is known as 'flexible specialization' in the US and as 'neo-Fordism' in France. Its underlying principle appears to be as significant as that of mass production introduced by Henry Ford in the early years of the twentieth century,[7] in an attempt to intensify the speed of work and thereby to reduce average costs.

The cost advantages to corporate managers of this system of decentralization are indeed enormous. The smaller the firm, the greater the scope for avoiding employment, labour and factory legislation. Moreover, in smaller units, the extent of unionization is relatively slight. The degree of unionization, again, is related positively to the incidence of organized industrial disputes. In the UK, the statistics indicate that factories of over 2,000 workers are 50 times more vulnerable to strikes than those with fewer than 100 workers. Moreoever, in a smaller business, the possibilites of using illegal employment practices, such as child labour and the evasion of tax and national insurance payments, are greater. In a study of the clothing and textiles industries, the Italian economist Luigi Frey found that small firms, by making use of insecure workers, were achieving savings in labour costs equal to about 14 per cent of the average output per worker.[8] Subcontracting provides a way of avoiding the costs associated with the benefits that labour has managed to win from capital, through years of militant struggle.

In the zealous promotion of small firms by monetarist governments in the UK and the US, there is, understandably, a strong ideological undercurrent. The privatization of the state sector in the Thatcherite UK has been guided by similar ideals. The small-scale sector in Europe has been generally promoted as a solution to unemployment and economic decline. It has also been viewed as an effective way of rekindling the entrepreneurial spirit. But one cannot fail to notice that the championing of this sector is, to a very large extent, based on the belief that labour is weaker in small firms than in large. The eulogy of the sector is also based on the perceived need to strengthen a class of small proprietors for social and political as well as for economic reasons. To quote Robin Murray, the small business strategy is really 'a class strategy, designed to weaken organized labour in large enterprises and to strengthen a petit-bourgeoisie which had been in long term decline'.[9]

The phenomena of sweatshops and homeworking can be viewed as logical extensions of the small business sector. In Italy, *lavoro nero* (the black economy), according to the *Financial Times* special report on Italy (26 March 1984), accounts for at least 30 per cent of the manufacturing output. If the underground economy is not as large as that in other OECD countries, there are indications that its size is alarmingly on the increase. The shift from the open or regulated to the hidden or unregulated economy is an essential feature in the industrial restructuring of most mature capitalist countries today.[10] This shift is by its very nature difficult to quantify, and that makes it easy for the pro-capital policymakers to ignore it. Although the potential loss of tax revenue is high, the shift may still be welcome, as it disperses the workers to fragmented production units. These invisible workers do not organize themselves in wage-bargaining or strikes, and therefore provide the ideal workforce for corporations involved in worldwide oligopolistic competition.

The hierarchy of subcontracting, in which the sweatshop economy and homeworking provide the last links, is the pivotal point of today's organizational changes. Contractors to TNCs put out work as much as possible to subcontractors, who in turn put out as much as possible to the next in the chain. Each company, however big or small, tries to minimize its involvement with the production process. The Italian *impannatori*, the middlemen, epitomize a process whereby the role of a firm becomes primarily financial and commercial, i.e. buying the inputs and/or selling the finished products.

Technological changes and the peripheralization of workers

The economic, rather than organizational, advantage of subcontracting is that it reduces the overhead costs of the hoarding
and training of labour. In order to reduce the fixed costs to a
minimum, the production strategy of companies is to invest in
permanent labour (and machinery) at a level just sufficient to
meet the expected demand. This is particularly so if any sudden,
unexpected or seasonal increase in demand can be conveniently
met by putting work out. Such a strategy is especially sensible in a
society where organized labour makes it difficult to achieve flexibility of labour through redundancies. This explains why putting-out became particularly popular in Italy after the 'hot
autumn' of 1969, when workers gained many concessions from
companies in terms of job security and working hours.

Fergus Murray describes the rationale of the organizational restructuring of a precision engineering firm in Bologna, with reliance on subcontracting:

> It . . . appears that [after 1969] a decision was taken to limit
> employment in the firm as militancy on the shopfloor in-
> creased and to cover rising demand by massively raising
> putting-out. In 1972, 46% of production work was put out
> of the firm, employing indirectly the equivalent of 570 full-
> time workers in small firms and workshops, whereas in
> 1969 only 10% had been put-out. In 1974–5 production fell
> rapidly, and work put out dropped to almost nothing, re-
> sulting in the loss of approximately 550 jobs. That is, while
> the level of employment in the firms working for the com-
> pany went through a massive fluctuation, employment in
> the company was relatively stable. The company putting
> the work out did not then pay a penny of redundancy
> money, nor was there any disruptive or socially em-
> barrassing struggle over the job losses.[11]

The shedding of labour on the factory floor has been expedited
by institutional changes as well. In Italy, large companies are
making extensive use of the so-called *cassa integrazione* (a fund
offering compensation for staying at home), which is being finan-

ced mainly by the government. Under the terms of the fund, the workers can be laid off 'temporarily' if the government agrees that the company is in a state of crisis. During such a period the workers are paid at slightly less than their normal wages from the fund. The arrangement can last up to five years. Half a million workers are in receipt of money from the *cassa integrazione* in Italy today, and large companies like Fiat, Olivetti and Montedison are regular users of this fund for laying off workers. In the automobile section of Fiat alone, nearly 30,000 workers lost their jobs between 1981 and 1984. The immense rationalization took momentum from the time of the strike at Fiat in 1980, which arose out of the dispute over the proposed cuts in jobs. The management finally won the battle thanks to a march through Turin by 40,000 Fiat workers, insisting, in defiance of the union, on their right to work.[12]

The shedding of labour has been achieved in large factories in Europe and America through the massive introduction of automation. Flexible manufacturing systems have expedited the process whereby robots and automatic machines can be linked together and run from a central computer system. Fiat's investment in automation, for example, has become a legend in the field of robot technology. The LAM engine assembly plant and the Robogate body plant are both run by highly flexible and intelligent robots devised by Comau, Fiat's equipment manufacturing subsidiary. The new automated system requires small groups of people, working in stations rather than on the assembly line, and who can change from one task to another at their own pace within specified targets set for the group as a whole. A very small multi-skilled core workforce alongside the robots has produced an employment structure where Fiat can proudly announce the delivery of cars that are 'hand-made by robots'. A more accurate description would be to say, perhaps, that they deliver cars which are 'assembled by robots', because a substantial number of the components are produced by the subcontractors in and around Turin working specifically to meet the production requirements of Fiat.

Indeed decentralization is the complementary strategy to automation – both aim to reduce the size of the workforce on the factory floor. The direction of technological changes since the 1970s has facilitated the process. The concept of the scale of production has changed considerably with the advent of new technology. Even in heavy industries such as cars or steel, it is no longer necessary to plan large-scale integrated production on the same factory floor. The introduction of modular designs in particular has made decentralization or putting-out feasible even in the most unlikely industries.

Such modular designs imply the standardization of the major subassembled parts of a product. Once standardized, each module can be made in different factories – possibly by subcontractors – and can then be put together, largely by robots, in the main plant. Already 40 per cent of the parts of Fiat's Ritmo model are being subassembled outside Fiat's factory in Turin. As the managing director of the car division says, 'What we have done is to transfer employment from Fiat to outside companies.'[13]

Another boost to decentralization has been given by the miniaturization of machines and tools – a direct consequence of the microchip revolution. The printing industry is a prime example. Traditional methods of typecast composition involved linotypes, monotypes or hand-compositions, whereby operators cast or picked out metal letters. Handsetting required substantial quantities of metal types, which are expensive and bulky to store. With the arrival of computer technology, the spatial concept of the industry has changed. Photocomposition has replaced the traditional kind of compositor's work. Instead of metal type, there are now keyboards that record the text, tapes or discs that store it, and a visual unit that displays it. The computer also has a photo-unit to produce film or printed photographs instead of plate-making. The minimal table-space that the new printing operation occupies has opened up the possibility of reducing the trade to a cottage industry. The scope has been increased by the fact that the cost of printing-units went down by more than 50 per cent in the 10 years after 1973.[14] At the cheapest end of the market, one can get a computerized printing-unit for around £3,000. In addition, software packages have been developed to meet the special needs of small printers. These miniaturization and modularization processes have also contributed to a changing gender structure of employment, by making the male muscle-power and zealously guarded craft-skills, traditional in industries such as printing, clearly superfluous.

On account of these technical changes, the West is now experiencing fundamental industrial restructuring. The shift towards marginalized workers is no longer confined to textiles, clothing and footwear, where the tradition of sweatshops, home-based work and small-scale production units has always existed. The phenomenon is increasingly spreading to technically more sophisticated industries. As Phil Mattera observed in the Italian context: 'Women in Turin were turning out parts for Fiat subcontractors on basement premises, in the region of Umbria they were fabricating miniature motors for teleprinters.'[15]

In short, technological progress has finally made it possible to disperse the factory proletariat into small plants and sweatshops where capital accumulation is possible without the restraints imposed by organized labour. The rate of exploitation can also be intensified without having to fear militancy. As a worker from Fiat's Lingotto pressed steel plant said in 1978:

> Small is hardly beautiful when you are working in one of the 70 firms with 30–50 employees that make parts of Fiat's decentralized bodywork, where you work Saturdays and do 10–12 hours overtime each week.[16]

Flexibility and control: the case of Benetton

In some other industries, such as clothing and electronics, microchips have affected the reassignment of labour processes in a different way. In these areas, it has been possible to split up the different sequences of production so that unskilled and repetitive parts can be relegated either to smaller units under the same management or to outside subcontractors. In such a situation a firm loses its central factory and becomes an agglomeration of 'detached workshops', that are located within or outside the national boundary.

The sequential breaking-up of the production processes made

these industries the focal point of the international division of labour in the 1970s, when an increasing amount of the repetitive, labour-intensive work was being sent to the Third World. In spite of this well-publicized trend, much of the labour-intensive work stayed in the advanced economies, where peripheralization of workers through increased layers of subcontracting became the major strategy for reducing costs.

It may be of some importance here to analyse the procedures that Benetton, the Italian clothing company, has used to increase its share in a highly competitive fashionwear market. In view of the publicity that the management strategies of Benetton have received in the last two years in the UK, it may not be unrealistic to assume that the company's policies are being flaunted in Britain as a model for others to emulate.[17]

Essentially a family business, this company experienced a phenomenal success within five years. In 1978, its jeans, jerseys and T-shirts were on sale at a few hundred shops in Italy, but exports were nil and turnover was a respectable but far from dazzling L66 billion (£30 million). Yet by 1983 Benetton was expecting to sell several times as much in money terms – L480 billion worth – through 2,500 shops. The Benettonization of the globe has included all the major cities of West Germany, America and even Japan. Luciano Benetton, the 49-year-old director of the company, has been named as Italy's fifth most successful director, and the UK's *Financial Times* has hailed him as 'the man who fashioned a clothing empire'.[18]

Particularly significant for the success of his strategies is the maximum combination of control and flexibility – control over marketing and retailing, and flexibility in production. Ascertaining the impulses of fashion is done with great sophistication and with the help of new technology. It is appreciated by the company that the key to the 'fast fashion' business is the ability to gauge the market and swiftly meet demand. The organizational policies are positively directed that way:

Housed in . . . Villa Orba, in a succession of clinically white rooms, is the heart of a complex information network that will eventually be linked to a computerized cash till in each shop, even those as far away as Washington and Tokyo. Every outlet will transmit detailed information on sales daily to headquarters to speed up the usually long-winded popular lines. If orange sells out in New York, Benetton will be asked to dye and supply replacement knitwear in half the manual time.

To speed the delivery, Benetton has commissioned Comau, the Fiat subsidiary that manufactures industrial robots, to build an automated warehouse near Ponzano . . . It will be manned by two technicians, each of whom, aided by an army of 13 robots, will be capable of emptying and loading a juggernaut in 30 minutes.[19]

It all amounts, as Luciano Benetton says, to raising fashion from the artisanal to the industrial level. But this is only as far as the marketing and related organizational changes are concerned. The centralization of marketing activities stands in sharp contrast to the decentralization of production activities. Although Benetton has eight factories in northern Italy, its payroll is less than 2,000. But it gives work to another 6,000 people – those who work for 200 small makers of semi-finished clothes, also in northern Italy, who supply Benetton's main plants. These small artisanal firms, in turn (like ethnic sweatshops in Britain), rely on a familial network for recruitment of female machinists, who work either on the floor of a small factory or from home.

The skilled parts of the production process – designing, dyeing, cutting and final ironing – are handled by Benetton, but most of the basic weaving and making-up is done outside the company's plants. The rationale is obvious: 'Benetton thus holds down its overheads, avoids the thankless task of managing a vast workforce and benefits from the much lower costs of the small subcontractors.'[20]

In many ways, Benetton epitomizes the current as well as the potential future use of NT in the oligopolistic capitalism of the garment industry in western Europe. NT increases the power of the big and successful companies to expand their market share by allowing them to respond speedily and efficiently to a change in market demand. But NT also facilitates the scope of subcontracting through a more effective fragmentation of the production process: the unskilled operations of 'shell-making' can be relegated to subcontractors, while the company retains complete managerial control over the designing, cutting and finishing of garments.

Race and gender: divisions in the hidden economy

As is obvious from the discussion above, the small business sector, closely tied to the large corporations by an invisible thread, subsumes a variety of subcontracting and different degrees of casualization of labour. Indeed the picture that emerges is far from homogeneous. It would be ludicrous to equate the working conditions in a small-scale foundry with those in a minuscule sweatshop. But amid the plethora of labour organizations presenting dissimilar sizes and types of units, a definite stratification on the basis of race and gender tends to emerge.

In the much-discussed black economy of Italy, for example, the white male workers enjoy the privileged position of being able to 'moonlight' while having a regular job. Similarly, skilled workers in minifirms, as well as artisans, are almost exclusively white males. So are the *impannatori* – the middlemen between the companies and the workers. In contrast, as Phil Mattera has documented, the women, the young, and the migrants from South Italy and North Africa are concentrated in the dirtiest, most precarious and worst-paid jobs.[21]

The division along the lines of race and gender permeates 'sunrise' industries just as much as traditional ones like clothing and textiles. In Japan, electric works such as wiring and the assembly of circuit-boards have proved so suitable for subcontracting that there are 180,000 women working as outworkers in the electrical component industry alone.[22] In the semiconductor industry of Silicon Valley in California, the division on the basis of race is just as marked as that on the basis of gender. In the high-tech valley of Santa Clara, which has the largest number of PhDs and millionaires per acre, the production line depends entirely on poorly paid women workers. The 500-odd electronic companies in Silicon Valley employ 200,000 people. Some 70,000 of these are women and they make up the bulk of the production work-force on the factory floor. Of the women production workers, 45 to 50 per cent are estimated to be from the Third World, particularly newly arrived Asian immigrants. These are the legal immigrants. Apart from the 200,000 or so officially recorded workers, undocumented immigrants are employed as well, though only in a 'black labour market' where payments are made in cash and the work gets done in sweatshops or at workers' homes. The cottage industry in Silicon Valley makes use of these poorest and most vulnerable workers for the labour-intensive parts of the electronic industry, for pay as low as 50 cents per piece. They may be a family working in its own home, usually on work subcontracted from smaller electronic companies. Alternatively, they may be 'hired' to work in garage sweatshops set up by a housewife or a middleman. Some of the larger electronic multinationals, too, are known to subcontract work to outworkers and sweatshops through intermediaries.[23] In fact, a key element in this high-tech world has been the spread of the 'pre-industrial' practices of cottage industries: industrial work is carried out in workers' homes, often in contravention of safety and health standards. The resurrection of this mode of production is also playing a major role in determining the pattern of international migration of labour as well as of capital.

Naomi Katz and David S. Kemnitzer assess the significance of recent trends in the US in this perspective:

> Although it is easier to move capital than people, the current internationalization process has not only relocated managerial and technical personnel abroad, but has encouraged widespread immigration to the US, including large numbers of 'unskilled' Asian women – a dramatic reversal of recent US immigration policies and something of an anomaly in these times of accelerating domestic unemployment.[24]

The creation of Third World enclaves in the middle of the First has proved beneficial to other industries as well, and has led to a new trend in capital restructuring in the big cities of America. A good example is the garment industry, whose general decline in the States has been well documented. Against an overall loss of jobs in this area in the US, the garment industry in New York's Chinatown has been growing since the late 1970s. While in 1970 there were approximately 180 garment factories in Chinatown, by the late 1970s there were 400. And these figures exclude sweatshops and homework. To quote Saskia Sassen-Koob, 'there is a growing awareness in the industry that wages in New York city are increasingly competitive with those in the garment industry in South-east Asia.'[25] This downgrading of wages is linked with the changing pattern of immigration to cities like New York and Los Angeles, where, since the late 1960s, the shift has been from a preponderance of immigration from high-wage European countries to one from low-wage countries of the Third World. Along with that, there has been a massive intake of un-documented Latin American and Caribbean immigrants. The estimates of such immigrants vary from six to 12 million, and the number is 'swelling by the hour'.[26]

These undocumented workers form the underclass that provides the cheapest labour. As a result, unlicensed sweatshops are springing up in all big cities such as Los Angeles, New York and Boston. Exact numbers are difficult to estimate, as the sweatshops tend to operate illegally on the fringes of the economy, in order to avoid unemployment insurance, minimum wage-rates, and regulations concerning child labour and overtime pay. The average wage can be 80 cents or less per hour. For an undocumented worker it can be difficult to demand and receive even that. The veiled threats of deportation for workers who do not possess 'green cards' prevents them from making trouble even when they are not paid their wages.[27]

Black women and outworking: the European scene

As in the States, the growth of the sweatshop economy in Europe has been alarmingly high in the last 10 years, and has been the direct result of relocation of some of the manufacturing industry from the Third World to the First. With the rise of unemployment in Europe, it has been possible and profitable for the large companies to have access to cheap and disposable labour near their markets, particularly labour in the shadowy area of the unregulated economy.

In spite of the spread of the sweatshop economy, very little research and documentation have been undertaken in this area by professional academic researchers. In the political climate of today, where the unfettered working of market mechanisms is positively encouraged, government research in the UK for instance, has consistently 'proved' that 'manufacturing homework is a relative rarity', and is only a stereotype left over from the last century.[28] This claim, needless to say, contradicts the experience of activists on the ground as well as that of grassroots researchers. It is precisely thanks to these researchers that we have a glimpse of the spread and implications of such a phenomenon.

Fear and desperation are the two major ingredients of the sweatshop economy. In it, therefore, poor working-class and black women provide the major input of labour. The weaker the bargaining position of workers, the keener employers become to engage them. As the *Annual Report of Greenwich Homeworkers Project* in 1984 explains:

> Employers know full well the situation of most of the women who come to them: they know that these women are desperate for money, can't find other work because of children or lack of skills, and are probably claiming benefit, so that they are not likely to cause them trouble by demanding higher wages.

Homeworkers and other workers in the sweatshop economy are almost invariably afraid. They are insecure: not knowing the boundaries of the law, they feel they are infringing the rules of officialdom. It is difficult for them to come out in the open. In the words of a British outworker:

> I do not think the authorities encourage people to be honest and declare their work. In my case, my husband is on a very low wage, so we are in receipt of Family Income Supplement. So I work to help pay for children's shoes etc but whatever I earn is deducted off FIS so in actual fact I end up working for nothing. To me it seems there is no way out of

the poverty trap, as the more I earn, the more is deducted from FIS.[29]

The very insecurity of their position forces such women to accept wages and working conditions that are reminiscent of the Victorian era. Sheila Allen's committed research in Bradford in the early 1980s vividly documents the plight of women homeworkers. A widow of 32 with four children describes her work:

> They [the children] all help, though not together, I don't allow it. I pay them, ½p for turning teddy [bears] and 2p for packing them. I'd rather work outside, the pay is better and I have always done it. But now [homeworking] just helps to buy their clothes and an occasional treat.[30]

This woman at the time worked for 20 hours a week and, with four children helping, earned £16.50.

Declining social facilities for childcare and for the care of the elderly make it difficult for many women to find jobs outside their homes, especially at a time when work is scarce. Hence, the earnings from home-based work, however meagre they may be, are a welcome addition for most poor families; often these are the only earnings that keep them above the poverty line. Male members of an impoverished family encourage women to take on homeworking; this way their work does not conflict with their perceived role as the carer of the family. As one homeworker says: 'Oh, no, they don't object to me working as long as I can be home to get their tea.'[31]

Constrained by their responsibility and expectations at home, women provide the ideal captive labour for the subcontractors of large companies. There is a startling similarity in the experience of homeworkers in Europe, which can be seen even in the limited number of studies that have been undertaken so far. Anneke Van Luijken of Tilburg, in the Netherlands, like Sheila Allen in the UK, has assiduously recorded the extent and the types of homeworking in her home town, that has experienced one of the highest rates of unemployment in the 1980s. With the collapse of the woollen and textiles industry that traditionally provided work in the town, the jobs disappeared at an unprecedented rate.

In their place, there was an increased supply of homeworking in the town, covering a wide range of products – from lampshades to links for machine-guns! The wages varied, and at times could be as low as the equivalent of 50 pence per hour. Most of the women workers were afraid to talk, as they could not afford to lose their jobs. Their earnings from homeworking provided a major input into family budgets. As Anneke Van Luijken documents:

> They often said to me: I don't mind telling you everything; it's honest money we work for. I only hope you don't mention my name in your article. I could not lose these extra earnings.

In an economic climate where an indigenous white woman is afraid to lose her homeworking job through publicity, immigrant women have to be extra careful. Hence, it is extremely difficult for an outsider to have even a glimpse of their working conditions. Anneke Van Luijken's experience was quite revealing:

> Many wives of foreign workers carry out homeworking. It was very difficult to get in touch with them. The language formed a barrier, but they were also more frightened and suspicious. Eventually I managed to get in touch with one of them . . . she lived on the first floor of a badly-built block of flats that dates from the sixties. Downstairs and on the staircase many foreign children were playing. A girl of about 12 opened the door. 'Wait,' she tells us and goes back. When we look inside, we see a woman working behind a tiny machine. We know she is making links for machine-gun bullets. The girl returns and tells us her mother is not at home.[32]

The ethnic economy

This urgency for immigrant women to remain invisible as workers in the intensely hostile and racist Europe of the 1980s has led to the most disturbing development, in the form of ethnic sweatshops. They now form an inalienable part of the inner-city phenomenon, although their existence hardly gets registered in the official statistics. Immigrants who came from the Mediterranean periphery and former colonies, to meet the demand for cheap labour during the post-war reconstruction period, had to find a new way of surviving in the changed situation when jobs from the factories and foundries disappeared. The recent statistics reflect an unusual rise in the level of self-employment among immigrants, and this phenomenon has not gone unnoticed by scholars either. Professor Boissevain at the University of Amsterdam, for example, has taken up this new role of the ethnic petit-bourgeois as an academic concern, in order to correct the radical perspective that so far has focused only on migrant workers.[33]

It would be a delusion, however, to believe that self-employment among black and immigrant communities in Western Europe at the moment is a springboard for upward economic and social mobility; in most cases, it is a symptom of utter desperation. Being excluded from the primary job market, black workers can rely on the sole advantage they have over their white counterparts – an easy access to flexible and cheap labour among the female members of their own community, available for work in the shadowy area between the regulated and unregulated economy.

Setting up one's own business, for most black entrepreneurs, therefore, is a sideways transition from 'lumpenproletariat to lumpenbourgeoisie'. Even as workers their position was highly marginalized; the treatment from fellow-workers was not conducive to class solidarity either. Patrick Duffy gave vivid documentation of the position of immigrant workers in a white-owned clothing factory in the East End of London in 1979:

> The factory was divided into three separate sections, each in its own building. One of these buildings was used as a cutting room, where there were six white cutters. The cutters were weekly paid. Another building, with perhaps 40 to 45 workers, performed the specialist machining, finishing, and top pressing functions, producing the racks of garments ready for dispatch. These workers were racially mixed, with perhaps half of them Bengalis. The employer said they were weekly paid.
> The third building, the 'machine room', was occupied by

about 45 young Bengalis, all engaged in flat machining ready-cut work from the cutting room, which was later passed to the finishing room. The premises belonged to the employer, the machines belonged to the employer, the work belonged to the employer, but none of these Bengali machinists were actually employed by the firm.

They were divided into several 'units', each with one of the Bengalis as a 'governor', who was responsible for negotiating for batches of the ready-cut work on a sub-contract basis from the cutting room. These machinists were paid on a piece-work basis, by their respective 'governors'. The 'employer' has no legal responsibility for any of these workers.

Asked what happened when there was a shortage of work, the 'employer' replied that it was not his problem: 'that is up to them', he said. As they were not employed by him, he did not have to make them redundant. If there was no work, there was no employment.

The white workers were incessantly suspicious of the Bangladeshi workers:

. . . the white cutter complained that the Bengalis claimed tax allowance for their children in Bangladesh. Somewhat inconsistent with this remark was his further claim that 'they don't pay tax' . . . The man further contradicted himself when he remarked that 'they have accountants who come in . . . but they are Indian too'.[34]

In this hostile environment, the obvious survival-strategy of the immigrants was to set up on their own, utilizing the safe inputs of ethnic and family labour.

The workers in the ethnic sweatshop economy are mostly women, but the entrepreneurs are invariably men. The traditional values of the immigrant communities, and the difficulty of finding jobs outside their own community, create a unique dependency relationship between the women and their ethnic employers, from whom they are often compelled to accept exploitative wage rates, ethnic ties notwithstanding. In terms of payment and job security, there is very little difference between working in smaller, often unregistered, companies and working from home. The women are never clear about their status as employees, and the questions of taxation and national insurance contributions are seldom raised.

It is not a coincidence that those ethnic communities which are particularly concerned with the 'Ijjat' or honour of their women are most successful in setting up on their own. In the confines of their community, employment is seen as a traditional obligatory relationship rather than a pure contract. The working conditions at the factory are seen as an extension of home life. As an Asian employer in the UK views the situation:

> I see the majority of women working for me as benefiting from my job offer. They are all illiterate and have no skills, hence no British factory will make use of them . . . I see myself providing a little extra for them: a place of work where they meet women in similar situations as themselves. Their £20 a week will help towards the family income, and we are like a big family here.[35]

Although working for a capitalist economy, the workers in the sweatshop economy are thus tied to their employers by an extra-economic bondage. In a hostile world, many of the immigrant women are afraid to incur the wrath of their own men. A woman may find it difficult to find alternative work if she is identified as a disruptive or unionized element. The servility, subservience and passivity that the communities expect of wives towards their husbands, daughters-in-law towards fathers-in-law in the home is reproduced to an important extent in factories. Since women are recruited through friends or relations, a direct telephone call to a husband, father or uncle is often enough to suppress rebels. Ethnic employers have also turned to their own associations (such as the Dressmakers and Allied Contractors Association among Cypriots in London), that are used to control the female labour force effectively.[36] Trapped between the racism of the host community and the sexism of their own, women of the ethnic minorities offer the advantage of Third World labour in the middle of the First.

Analysing the response of 50 homeworkers in the clothing

Islamic patriarchy in an alien land

The recourse to Islam is basically a refuge, a dam to keep one's roots and origins safe. Islam takes the place of language, culture and identity. It is opposition to what comes from without – in this case, the immediate environment, thought of as what is foreign. It is the major point of reference and the ready-made answer to complex and varied questions. A culture detached in this way from the land and people where it lives and evolves soon finds itself reduced to an expression of reaction – not necessarily positive. It is perceived as a veil one tries to put over a wound, over problems that make one afraid. Thus Maghreb parents have exaggerated their attachment to Islam and to the traditions of their native land, in order to counter the temptations that attract their children, alienating them and making strangers of them. . .

It is young girls especially who suffer most from this oppression. . . The daughter of immigrants lives an exile within exile . . .

. . . Despite having been uprooted, Maghreb men try to keep alive the social pressures that determine the relations between men and women in their native land. It is a way of expressing their attachment to the ancestral culture.

Source: Tahar Ben Jelloun, *Hospitalité française*, Paris: Seuil 1984, pp. 105–10.

industry in Leicester in 1981, it was found that wages ranged from 10 pence to £2.50 per hour; the average rate per hour was only 80 pence, and that did not allow for expenses such as electricity, heating, depreciation of the machines, or the time spent cleaning after each day's work.[37] A breakdown of costs by the West Midlands Low Pay Unit in 1984 shows that a garment selling at £11.99 in high street shops gives the retailers a £6.00 profit and an Asian machinist between 15 and 75 pence, depending on the difficulty of the work done and whether it is carried out in a factory or at home. On average, in small sweatshop units in the West Midlands, a typical wage is around £1.00 per hour, but for homeworkers it can be much lower than this.[38] According to trade sources, not even Hong Kong or Taiwan can compete at this level of pay.

It is not surprising, therefore, that in many manufacturing industries, such as clothing, footwear and toys, there are now obvious trends towards moving production back from the Third World to western Europe. In some sectors of the clothing industry, such as women's fashionwear, imports have been virtually halted. In the UK, a quick trip to new and successful chains such as Next, Solo, or Principles would reveal that the days are gone when the majority of merchandise came from South-east Asia. Now it is not only Marks and Spencer that can boast of selling British.

The curious fact is that this increased volume (and value) of domestic output has not been accompanied by increased levels of employment. In the United Kingdom, official statistics in fact show a steady decline in employment in the traditional sectors such as clothing, implying an increase in the average labour productivity (Figure 4). It does not seem logical, however, to ascribe the rise in output to the improved productivity of existing workers, when investment in machinery has been declining dramatically since 1974, reaching an all-time low in 1982. This fall in investment has also been accompanied by a pronounced proliferation of small units of production in the last five years. In the West Midlands alone, there has been a growth of at least 400 such sweatshop units. Increased productivity, therefore, could not have arisen out of an overall rationalization of the industry, since that would have implied a concentration of products in a small number of large and efficient firms. The answer to the paradox of increased production with falling employment is that there has been a major shift of employment and production from the regulated to the unregulated sector. Increased output has simply increased the volume of work allotted to homeworkers and workers in sweatshop units at the expense of factory employment.

The growth of the unregulated or hidden economy becomes an important feature of the current industrial restructuring in the West, as capital increasingly comes home. Homeworking in the hidden economy, in this context, cannot be viewed as an isolated phenomenon: it is the ultimate form of flexible employment that management demands.

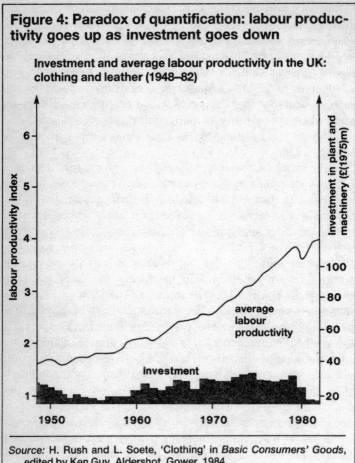

Figure 4: Paradox of quantification: labour productivity goes up as investment goes down

Investment and average labour productivity in the UK: clothing and leather (1948–82)

Source: H. Rush and L. Soete, 'Clothing' in *Basic Consumers' Goods*, edited by Ken Guy, Aldershot, Gower, 1984.

The clothing industry in the UK

The role of homeworking in the global economy, therefore, can be understood only with reference to a chain of subcontracting that links home-based female workers to the business strategies of the global corporations. In a number of industries, multinational companies dominate not through their control over production, but entirely through their monopoly over marketing. The clothing industry in the UK typifies such a pattern of control. The majority of retail sales in the garment industry are now controlled by no more than a dozen chain stores, such as Marks and Spencer, C & A, British Home Stores and Littlewoods. Marks and Spencer is the largest of them and accounts for nearly a fifth of all garments sold in the country. The large corporations that monopolize the retail market do not produce a single item; they are often, quite aptly, described as the 'manufacturers without factories'.

The description is particularly pertinent in view of the hold the companies have over those who manufacture for them, who are fragmented and depend entirely on the big retail companies for their custom. Nearly 600 suppliers cater to the demands of Marks and Spencer alone. In the inner-city areas, where production of fashion clothes usually takes place, there is a preponderance of small units of production. Over 80 per cent of employment in London's clothing industry is accounted for by firms employing fewer than 50 people.

The specific nature of the garment industry has given rise to a very special relationship between retailers and manufacturers in the UK, whereby the former can 'dictate not only the number of stitches and the width of hem, but also the profit margins of those from whom they buy'.[39] Threats of sourcing overseas keep the margin low. As one of the Marks and Spencer suppliers describes it, the diktat of the retailers to the manufacturers in the UK 'has similarities to the traditional address by a Sergeant Major to his new recruits: you play ball with me and I will play ball with you'.[40]

The unequal relationship between the retailers and the manufacturers places the latter at a definite disadvantage. In the early 1980s, when the market slumped as a result of recession, the retailers waged a price war against one another in order to secure a substantial share of the shrinking market. The real cost of the price war, however, had to be borne mainly by the manufacturers, as the retailers demanded that their suppliers shoulder half the burden of the price cuts. Under such pressures, for the small manufacturers that managed to survive, the long-term effects on profit margins were serious and demanded drastic changes in strategy. The options open to the manufacturers were stark: to reduce the overhead costs by increased use of part-time and temporary workers, to engage in fictitious liquidation of companies, or to pass the overhead costs to the next down in the chain of subcontracting. Thus a greater reliance on vulnerable homeworkers became an important part of their strategy.

The introduction of microelectronic technology in the 1980s has not reversed the trend. If anything, technological changes have only intensified it. The implementation of microelectronic technology has been massive in distribution and marketing in the clothing industry; computers have in fact given managements the most effective tool to gauge the changes in fashion and to meet them promptly. By contrast, the implementation of microtechnology has been negligible in production.[41] With a large number of small producers seeking the custom of big retailers, it hardly makes sense to invest in expensive machinery, especially when changes in fashion are frequent and when a source of extremely cheap labour is at hand.

One of the most important changes that new technology has brought about in the clothing industry is that in some segments fashion has become more crucial than price-competitiveness. Flexibility in colour and design now holds the key to success. The result is that the number of different styles in garments appears to be increasing, as is the number of styles being discontinued from season to season. Where once maybe 5 per cent of the styles would be replaced, it can now be nearer 20 per cent or more. The strategy of cultivating fashion changes has become so endemic that even Marks and Spencer have had to rethink their policy in order to maintain their share in the market:

> Marks, always ready to acknowledge trading mistakes, said it was trying hard to shed its middle-of-the-road fuddy-duddy image. 'We welcome the Nexts, Benettons and the others and meet the challenge with confidence. We are determined to find an image.'[42]

In this volatile market, high street retailers (who unlike Benetton, are not responsible for their own production) prefer to source close at hand. It is difficult for the large-scale garment manufacturers in the Far East to be responsive, either in design or colour terms, or in speed of delivery, to the fashion requirements of a remote market. But most of all, ordering in advance from the distant corners of the world may involve retailers in the high cost of holding unsold stock of out-of-fashion clothes.

Preference for domestic sources has not, however, changed the power relationship between the retailers and the numerous suppliers. Retailers positively pursue multiple sourcing domestically. In this way, they maintain, if not encourage, the fragmented nature of the industry. For a large retailer, the existence of a particular small supplier is not of any great consequence. But the existence of a large number of them increases his bargaining strength.[43] The main contractors of the large retailers follow the same policy in their turn. As the number of subcontractors increases, the risks of fashion changes can be passed on to the next in the line. In smaller units factory and labour legislation can be conveniently avoided and, most important of all, in such units there is scant unionization. In the subcontracting network, ethnic entrepreneurs play an important role near the bottom of the chain. They provide the most flexible of all labour: their own women.

Black women and the labour movement

This confined labour market gives some immigrant male entrepreneurs a competitive advantage. It is considered 'normal' for an immigrant woman, on the other hand, to be just a worker: in her cultural milieu, it is often accepted as desirable for a woman to work – if not in a strictly supervised ethnic factory – from the confines of her home. Hence the ethnic economy throughout the UK is marked by a clear division of labour along gender lines. Unskilled, repetitive, machining work gets done by women – from small units or from home – whereas entrepreneurial skill is practised and monopolized by men.

The price that the immigrant women pay, in terms of health hazards and safety, is often high. Being for the most part un-

---

Homeworking: when fear eats the soul

When you live in Newham [London], you have little choice, sister. Burning down of an Asian home does not even make news any longer. It is accepted as a regular happening in the East End of London. The police are no help; they would not admit that the attacks on Asian homes are from the racists. How can I look for jobs outside my home in such a situation? I want to remain invisible, literally.

Also, sister, I am a widow and I really do not know what my legal status is. If I apply for cards and things, I may be asked to leave the country. At the moment, my uncle brings machining work to my home. It works out to be 50 pence per hour, not great! But I earn and I feed my children somehow. Most of all, I do not have to deal with the fear of racist abuse in this white world.

Source: Interview by the author taken in August 1985.

---

registered, they are likely to be unaware of any protection that the health and safety regulations offer. Nor are the workers in sweatshops in a better position. According to the present law, registration with the Factory Inspectorate is not needed. The fire service inspects factories only where more than 20 people are working. Accidents that result from working in sweatshops and homeworking accordingly affect mainly immigrant women. Incidents, such as that reported below, reveal a common pattern of organizing production and the dangers that may follow from it:

> Six members of an Asian family . . . died when an explosion and fire destroyed their home in Gravesend, Kent . . . The family had only moved from the Midlands some four months ago and were thought to be operating a small shoe manufacturing business from the premises . . . The victims were Jagir Kaur, aged 48, her daughter 19-year-old Disho Kaur, daughter-in-law Manjit Kaur and grandchildren . . . the blaze was intensified by quantities of glue, plastic and compressed air stores in the small workshop.[44]

This piece of news appeared a few days after the reporting of a similar accident in the East End of London:

The five women who died in a clothing factory fire in East London on Wednesday, worked in premises which had not been visited by fire prevention officers or factory inspectors . . . The factory, D. K. Netwar, of Mile End Road, was owned by members of an Indian family, including Mr Gurdev Singh. The dead women had not all been named last night but they were understood all to be Indians, some of whom might have been related to Mr Singh . . . Two of the victims were identified last night as sisters, Baksho and Vidya Kaur . . . [45]

It is not surprising, therefore, that women researchers are trying to make the issues of the sweatshops and homeworking visible. It is the invisibility of this particular form of labour process that makes the workers so pathetically vulnerable, and perpetuates the myth that homeworkers work only for pin money (Table 6).

The contribution of grassroots researchers in various homeworking groups in Europe has been invaluable in counteracting this myth. Most of their work in the last four or five years has been directed towards the exposure of the extent of homeworking, the low pay and the level of exploitation, as they have felt that this is just as important as pure quantification and playing the numbers game. They thought, understandably, that establishing solidarity with homeworkers was the necessary precondition for a valid quantification. The absence of a precise figure for the rise in manufacturing homework, however, makes it easy for officials to dismiss concern over the spread of homeworking as 'probably exaggerated'.

Yet the labour movement can ill afford to ignore the alarm that has been signalled by women's organizations. As my own quantification in *Capital and Class* shows, between 1978 and 1983 in the fashionwear sector of the clothing industry alone, the loss of jobs in the official sector resulting from a transference of work from the open to the hidden economy has been five times as great as that resulting from import penetrations.[46] The impact of such transference of jobs on the organized labour movement has also been dramatic. Between 1963 and 1983, membership of the Nat-

Table 6: A profile of eight Asian homeworkers (machinists) in Leicester (March–July 1982)

I.   Hours of work and earnings

Outworker	Average pay per hour	Hours per week	Average weekly pay	Deductions
1	23p	55-60	£12.50	Tax
2	40p	30-45	£15.00	Machine rental £4.00
3	£1.80	40-50	£72.00	–
4	70p	15-35	£14.50	Tax and NI
5	70p	30-35	£23.00	None
6	50p	80-90	£35.00	Machine rental £4.00
7	90p	30-35	£31.00	None
8	£2.00	30-40	£65.00	Tax and NI
Average Rates	**90p**	**48 hours**	**£33.50**	

Note: All homeworkers paid for their overheads: electricity, heating, lighting and telephone. Estimated cost is £5.00 a week on average.

II.   Patterns of Expenditure

Outworker	Average weekly income from outwork	Wages from outwork used for	Husband's weekly wage	Main items of expenditure (apart from normal household bills)
1	£12.50	Housekeeping	Not known	Mortgage
2	£15.00	Childrens clothes	Unemployment benefit	not known
3	£72.00	Everything – only income	Unemployed: not on benefit	not known
4	£14.50	Essentials	£75.00	Mortgage
5	£23.00	Essentials	£100+	Mortgage
6	£35.00	Essentials	£45.00	Mortgage Support for mother-in-law in Bangladesh £100 per month
7	£31.00	Clothes and essentials	£100+	Mortgage
8	£65.00	Savings	£95.00	Mortgage

Source: Work with Asian Outworkers: Report by Leicester Outwork Campaign 1982.

ional Union of Tailors and Garment Workers in the UK has fallen dramatically. Whereas the membership in the East End of London alone was 22,000 in 1963, the membership in the whole of south-east London 20 years later barely exceeded 5,000. Big clothing firms such as Simpson's, Burberry, Moss Brothers, Poliakoff, Hope Brothers have moved out of their East End factories; into their place have moved ethnic entrepreneurs, with their army of female workers providing cheap machinists.

Black women provide labour not only for the clothing but for many of the low-tech manufacturing industries, where the use of homeworking is likewise increasing. As the Greenwich Homeworkers' Project states, 'This invisible workforce provides the lampshades we buy from stores on the High Street, dresses, blouses, electrical goods, stuffed envelopes, painted toys, zips and many other goods.' In the absence of further resources to extend their investigations, the workers on the ground tend to feel that 'for every homeworker we talk to, there are many others we may never know'.

The numerical strength of homeworkers, however, seriously undermines the strength of organized labour movements. It is in the interests of organized labour as well as in the interests of black women that the mainstream labour movement should recognize and challenge the racist roots underlying the creation of such an underclass.

New technology homeworkers

The spread of homeworking is not confined to the manufacturing sector. New technology is increasingly making it possible to do most clerical, service and office work from workers' homes. A large part of office work is concerned with the storing, processing and transmission of information. With microcomputers, the information employers require can now be neatly stored in a computer system and retrieved at a traditional workplace, at a branch office in another part of the country or at home. The result is the rise of a new type of homeworker – remote-workers or 'teleworkers' – and again a majority of these are women.

A number of studies undertaken in France, Sweden, the US,

Canada and the UK indicate that a substantial part of secretarial as well as white-collar executive jobs can be effectively performed from home. In order to make teleworking possible, all that one technically needs, apart from the computer, is a remote terminal and the telephone grid to which it is connected. The spread of teleworking, therefore, depends entirely on the costs involved in the use of the telecommunications system and the computers. The availability of cheap home computers and microprocessor-based office equipment means that the only constraint affecting the widespread use of remote-working is the cost of transmission through telecommunication. But technological changes have been rapid in this direction as well. Ursula Huws summarizes the state of technology succinctly:

> While still slightly more expensive than the traditional coaxial copper cables, new optical fibre cables are much smaller in diameter, and capable of carrying a much greater number and range of signals, and their cost is tumbling fast. Together with the burgeoning satellite communications industry, which is also providing an even cheaper service, they can supply us with a worldwide fully interactive communication network, at a fraction of the price of traditional telecommunications systems.[47]

As the cost of communication comes down, it becomes increasingly more economical for management to transfer work, whenever it is possible, to domestic units. Experimentation with remote-working is under way in many countries. Banks in the US have connected transmission lines to keyboards in the home. The text comes by dictaphone, it is typed at home and appears on a printer in the bank. A number of large American corporations have been successfully using homeworkers for routine office work for a number of years. The names include Montgomery Ward, Arthur D. Little, Standard Oil of Indiana and the First National Bank of Chicago. The California-based Freight Data Systems, a firm which provides a database for shipping companies on freight rates, reported a satisfactory outcome to a homeworking experiment. The scheme was originally embarked upon as a solution to an office space problem. But the advantages were much greater than just saving the office space. The $1,700 per household which it cost to install the terminals and communication links was considerably cheaper than the cost of expanded premises and travelling expenses. Supervision problems were minimized by a bonus system which offers extra money to those who complete work in record time.[48] A combination of piece-rates and the absence of fringe benefits makes homeworking a most cost-effective way of getting clerical and office work done.

One can thus identify two important advantages to management arising from this new type of homeworking. First, the employer can save expensive overhead costs such as renting or buying prime office sites. Second, the company can benefit by changing the nature of its contractual obligations with the employees. This change involves a switch from 'wage payment for time worked' to 'fixed fees for work done'. This up-market piece-rate system thereby reduces the status of employees to self-employed, much to the advantage of the company. The employer does not have to be responsible for holiday pay, sick pay, national insurance contributions, redundancy payments or other ancillary benefits that are due to an employee. The intensity of work can be increased as well, by eliminating the time usually spent on social intercourse in a place of work.

The advantages of a contractual assignment are described by the management of Rank Xerox:

> We have looked at our costs in our headquarters building and have identified that someone who was paid, say, £10,000 was costing us something like £27,000 to employ. Of the total costs, 30 per cent went in salaries, 31 per cent went in facilities. A pretty even match. But if you convert the £10,000 salaries into fee payments you have greater control; fees, unlike salaries, invariably add value. You are paying someone to do something.[49]

The cost-effectiveness of remote-working is so great that companies like Rank Xerox encourage their senior and middle-ranking executives, with positive financial help, to set up as independent freelance consultants. The system is called 'networking', and is only one of many different ways of decentralizing executive and professional work to outside sources and home-based units. In France and Sweden, companies have tried the so-called neighbourhood centres. These are small work premises which are fully equipped with computer terminals, where individuals can hire space.

Teleworkers, therefore, can cover a whole range from secretarial and clerical workers to pension managers, market intelligence people, tax lawyers and other varieties of knowledge workers. In the words of Rank Xerox management: 'They are the people whose presence on our premises is not required all the time, as long as their spirit and brain are here.'

However, because the system covers a whole range of activities and skills, there is an inherent danger that the spread of new technology homework will reproduce the gender differentiation in work within the confines of the home. Instead of liberating a woman from the chores of a repetitive work pattern, NT will simply deprive her of the luxury of going out to work. She is likely to end up with the burden of a double day, trying to combine her domestic chores with her professional work.

One feels apprehensive to hear the praise of this new pattern of work as being particularly suitable for women, who are housebound by the need to care for their young children and disabled or elderly dependants. The flexibility of the system so easily provides an excuse for reducing the facilities for childcare, nurseries and geriatric hospitals. This mode of work inevitably increases the amount of unpaid work that an average woman does within the domestic unit.

The flexibility that the system offers to professional married women was in fact the primary reason behind the setting up in Britain of F-International, the software company, by its woman founder Steve Shirley, in 1962. In the decades since then, the company has grown into one of the leaders in the software field, with a staff of around 900, and with subsidiary companies in Denmark, Holland and the United States. In 1969, ICL followed the example of F-International: it currently employs nearly 200 home-based women workers, and has plans for further expansion. In both companies the homeworkers are computer professionals – systems analysts, programmers and technical authors.

In her 1982 survey of new technology homeworkers in the UK, Ursula Huws found that the majority of workers were women and all but five were parents, generally of pre-school children.[50] The picture that emerged, therefore, was that the typical new technology homeworker was 'a married woman in her mid-thirties who had chosen to be home-based in order to look after her family'. A systems analyst in Ursula Huws's survey summed up the dilemma that faces a woman concisely. She gave 'being with the children all day' as the main advantage of homeworking. Then, when asked what was the main disadvantage, she replied, 'being with the children all day'.[51] Isolation, non-unionization and uncertainty as to the status of their employment characterize women's unease in this form of work. But most of all, working from home deprives a woman of her professional image. The contrasting collective image of a male and a female homeworker, as projected by the media, is interesting to observe. In the context of French magazines, Elsbeth Monod notes:

> We have been amused to flick through magazines and newspapers where, for three years, articles for the general public have appeared on the theme. The illustrations that complement the texts represent women combining the 'feminine' professional activities with traditional domestic tasks. One notices the abundance of details where women telework – paper screens, flowery dress, wallpaper. It's a must to haul up the presence of children or the cot. The probable aroma of the cooking that could waft out of the kitchen. They also bring in the comments on hairstyle, unless it has been reduced to curlers. Observe the 'virile' decor in contrast which surrounds a man who teleworks – strict space, library, or in short, office at home. In conclusion, when a woman does her telework she does it in the dining room in the midst of all domestic paraphernalia that include the children. Whereas for a man teleworking at home, a particular area is converted into office.
>
> In summary, a woman loses her professionalism at home whereas a man preserves it.[52]

The contribution of NT need not be confined to the house-wification of service and office jobs within a national boundary. As cable technology makes it easy to move office jobs around within a national boundary, satellite technology is making it increasingly convenient to send similar jobs to offshore low-wage countries. Offshore information processing is already in vogue in America and the economic rationale behind it is clear. As the company chairman of Satellite Data Corporation, New York, claimed: 'We can do the work in St Michael's, Barbados, for less than it costs in New York to pay for the floor space.' The same logic has led American Airlines to close their data entry operation recently in Tulsa, Oklahoma, and hire 200 Barbadians to do the work instead. A satellite links the Barbados operation with Tulsa, Oklahoma. Most of the moves in office jobs so far have been from America, and have been destined for English-speaking ex-British colonies of the Caribbean or the Far East. But the trend is spreading, and by the end of the decade, with the improvement of satellite communications, as Ursula Huws observed, it will be just as simple and cost-effective to transfer information processing work between continents as it is to make a long-distance telephone call.[53]

With the advance of telecommunication technology, therefore, the runaway office jobs are following the same pattern as that of the runaway manufacturing jobs. The jobs in question, significantly, are extremely repetitive and labour-intensive. They are, to quote Ursula Huws, 'the sort of routine low-status office work which provides employment for thousands of women, from ethnic minorities, in the big cities of Europe and North America'.[54]

4. Women working worldwide

No farewell to the working class

A significant yet grossly underemphasized aspect of the current global restructuring is, as we have seen, the emergence of an acutely polarized labour market. In such a market, increasingly, a small number of core workers is going to co-exist with a vast array of peripheral workers. There are many names for these peripheral workers: flexible workers, casual workers, or, as in the context of Free Trade Zones, temporary or part-time proletariat. All these terms have the same or similar connotations, and conjure up invariably the image of a worker who is a woman, and whose status as a wage-earner does not necessarily carry with it an automatic prospect of career progression. Nor does the image imply job security or other employment-related benefits such as a core worker enjoys.

Who are these peripheral or casual workers? They work for small subcontracting firms, or are young recruits in the Free Trade Zone areas, where hiring and firing are easy. In larger companies, they provide services on a contract basis to meet sudden or seasonal upturns in demand. These predominantly female workers are called casual not because of a lack of commitment or experience on their part, but simply because their conditions of work have been deliberately casualized. They provide the base of a growing 'shoe-shine' economy even in the affluent West (Figure 5).

Equally striking is the creation of a small but highly privileged and multi-skilled elite of workers in corporate organizations. With a well-defined career path in a secure job, such workers are likely to identify themselves more with company ethics and corporate management than with casual workers. Significantly, the majority of core workers are men, and the trade unions still maintain commitment to their cause.

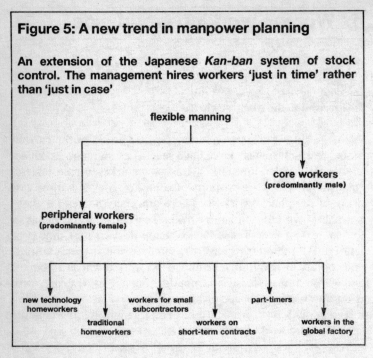

Figure 5: A new trend in manpower planning

An extension of the Japanese *Kan-ban* system of stock control. The management hires workers 'just in time' rather than 'just in case'

flexible manning

core workers
(predominantly male)

peripheral workers
(predominantly female)

new technology
homeworkers

traditional
homeworkers

workers for small
subcontractors

workers on
short-term contracts

part-timers

workers in the
global factory

The division of labour along these lines is influenced by the Japanese system of management; in fact, the system is an extension of the principle used by Japanese companies for a successful method of stock control. It is known as the 'kan ban' system, and implies having materials 'just in time' rather than 'just in case'. The principle is applied equally effectively by management to the problem of recruiting labour at the lowest possible cost.

This approach to manpower planning, novel in the West, has begun to change the composition of the working class. This change is becoming more pronounced with the growth of home-based work. Increasingly, the self-employed and the hidden workers of the 'sweatshop economy' complement the flexible workers of the 'shoe-shine economy'. Unfortunately, in spite of their growing numbers, they remain, like the flexi-workers on the factory floor, at the margin of the mainstream labour movement.

These changes imply that the working class no longer consists mainly of white male workers; instead, the concept 'working class' increasingly covers blacks, women, and in many sectors black women workers. This new working class is largely ignored not only by the mainstream labour movement but by most writers on economic and political issues. Whereas literally thousands of articles have been written on the labour-replacing aspect of new technology, only a handful have been written on the casualization of work, and these mostly by committed women scholars. Titles such as 'Collapse of work' or 'World without work' are commonplace on the library shelves. Videos also take up the theme: 'Chips are down', 'Mighty Micro', 'Chips with everything'. All these remind us of a future in which the inputs of human labour will be totally unnecessary for the production of goods and services. Concerned philosophers attempt to alter our world-view in order to help us come to terms with the changed material conditions of production. In his thought-provoking book *Farewell to the Working Class*, André Gorz, for example, looks forward longingly to the abolition of most kinds of work, which will usher in the 'non-class of non-workers', who are not conditioned to believe in the sacredness of work. His non-class, unlike the outmoded Marxist concept of the working class, is not a 'social subject': 'It has no transcendent unity or mission . . . it has no prophetic aura. Instead, it reminds individuals of the need to save themselves and define a social order compatible with their goals and autonomous existence.'[1] Striving towards this new social order would involve, according to Gorz, a coherent 'policy of time', which would involve reduction of working hours, and sharing of jobs. But most of all it would entail learning to appreciate the pleasures of unpaid jobs and being prepared to relinquish the right to paid jobs.[2]

This scenario does not appear plausible at present, when the major impact of new technology seems to be in the intensification of the work process through massive subcontracting and casualization of employment. Moreover, to strive for a future of this kind may not seem so attractive either, especially to millions of women workers. In fact, the 'labour of love' or 'unpaid work' is not a new experience to women. Society's expectation that

---

'Labour of love'

'Have you many children?' the doctor asked.

'God not has been good to me. Of 15 born, only nine live', he answered.

'Does your wife work?'

'No, she stays at home'.

'I see. How does she spend her day?'

'Well, she gets up at four in the morning, fetches water and wood, makes the fire and cooks breakfast. Then she goes to the river and washes clothes. After that she goes to town to get corn ground and buys what we need in the market. Then she cooks the midday meal'.

'You come home at midday?'

'No, no, she brings the meal to me in the fields – about three kilometres from home'.

'And after that?'

'Well, she takes care of the hens and pigs and of course she looks after the children all day . . . then she prepares the supper so it is ready when I come home'.

'Does she go to bed after supper?'

'No, I do. She has things to do around the house until about nine o'clock'.

'But of course you say your wife doesn't work?'

'Of course she doesn't work. I told you she stays at home'.

Source: International Labour Organization 1977.

---

women will provide such labour at home does not disappear even when they are in paid jobs. As a result, in market-oriented as well as in socialist countries, increased wage employment for women in the post-war years has almost invariably meant burdening women with two jobs.

In spite of the burden of a double day, however, most women would welcome the opportunity of going out to work, as only this gives credibility to their status as workers. The limited achievement of such credibility that women have gained in the last two decades has in fact been entirely due to the expansion of paid work outside the home, however exploitative. Not surprisingly, therefore, in a trade-off between the oppression of family life and the drudgery of ill-paid work, most women prefer the latter.

Ironically, it is the access to paid outside work which has given many women a chance to reclaim dignity for themselves in the domain of their own family lives. Unwaged hours of work, by general consensus, are seen as an extra-economic activity, however essential they may be for the productive sphere of a society. The hidden labour of women becomes unrecognized labour, and there is always a pressure not to subject this labour to the cool calculations of economic accounting. As André Gorz writes: 'Raising children, looking after and decorating a house, repairing or making things, cooking good meals . . . none of these activities is carried out for economic ends or for consumption.'[3]

Much to the chagrin of romantic visionaries, however, women's movements have adopted the strategy of demanding wages for housework. Alternatively, they demand greater social provision of care facilities for children and the old. This is because only by bringing some of these occupations out of the private sphere into the social domain have women in the West achieved some power in the political system. It is power of this kind that could be used effectively for an equitable distribution of work and leisure in tomorrow's society.

Indeed one looks with some trepidation at the glorification of the family, not only by the moral majority in America and the Thatcherites in the UK, but also by an iconoclast of the radical world such as Ivan Illich. He sees the sexual division of labour in and outside the home as based on 'vernacular gender', that is, on a natural complementarity which he claims is clearly visible in pre-industrial societies. To question it leads him to 'the conclusion that the struggle to create economic equality between genderless humans of two different sexes resembles the efforts made to square the circle with ruler and straight edge'.[4]

In Father Illich's natural order, it is the women who are to contribute most of the unpaid work, 'shadow work' as he calls it. For this type of work, women ought not to ask for remuneration, because 'the best they can hope for is not a shadow price but a consolation prize'.[5] In his bitter critique of the women's movement, Illich concludes that the demand to end sex discrimination is an idle luxury of elite women who have benefited somehow from economic growth:

> . . . the Mexican woman with the two-car garage leaves the
> house in charge of a domestic when she escapes to a femi-
> nist gathering . . . Her experience is totally beyond that of
> her distant cousin, who lives with the tooth puller in the
> village . . . The tooth puller's concubine still knows by
> magic and gossip how to keep men in their place. The bour-
> geois latina has traded both for the servant plus car, and the
> right to flirt with feminist rhetoric.[6]

A priest's vision of a womanly woman in her natural habitat is
a far cry from the vernacular women I know of, who frantically
search for paid employment to escape poverty, the oppression of
family life and bride-burning. In a world where one in three
families is headed by a woman, and where the number of such
families is increasing at an alarming rate, the idealized image of a
woman immersed contentedly in her 'shadow work', while her
vernacular hunter man brings the bacon home, ought to be confined only to a romantic's dream. It is the woman's urgency and
desire to work outside the home that have created a new working
class.

Women organizing internationally

The power of the stereotype dies hard. The myth of a male
breadwinner perpetuates a convention where it is considered just
for women to receive lower wages even when they perform similar jobs. So, too, it is considered 'natural' for women to accept
jobs which are part-time, temporary or performed in home-
based units. In the ideology of a patriarchal family unit, a
woman's primary role is considered to be in the area of domestic
work and in the care of children and older relatives. Hence her
commitment to paid work outside her home is seen by society
and by her family as less than perfect. However exacting her profession may be, however many hours she may put into her work,
a woman worker is always seen as a 'permanent casual'.

Indeed, because of the accepted notion of a 'natural' sexual
division of labour at home, the male members of a society tend to
view a woman's commitment to paid work as an aberration that

should be resisted. Such politics of gender within the family unit extend themselves to the conflict between male and female workers on the factory floor, thereby unwittingly giving TNCs an added power to counteract the challenge of the organized labour movement.

The common experience of male attitudes has brought about, especially in the 1980s, a sense of solidarity among female workers, a new awareness of a bond that transcends racial and geographical boundaries. The new technology has been instrumental in fragmenting the production process to the advantage of the TNCs, but it has also, by facilitating improved communication and transport, helped women workers to exchange their experiences. Feminist conferences on the labour movement in recent years bear testimony to this contribution of NT.

Here I shall document only a few such conferences, of which I have had personal experience, to illustrate the objectives and mechanism of establishing such worldwide networks. In October 1982, 26 women from the North and the South met at the Transnational Institute in Amsterdam, to consider together the communality as well as the divergences in their experiences as workers in the global clothing and textiles industry. In a colloquium that lasted over three days, the contributors included trade unionists and activists as well as committed researchers in this area. Not only were they all women, most of them were mothers of young children. Their concern with the political and economic issues was understandably interspersed with concern for the children or babies they left at home. One brought her young son with her, and women felt and showed deep sympathy for the delegate from the Philippines whose husband was in prison for his political activism against President Marcos. The participants were by no means the usual crowd one finds at an international conference. For some, this was the first visit away from their home and country. Women came from England, Scotland, Eire, Holland, Canada, the United States, Germany, India, the Philippines, the Mexican–American border, Hong Kong, Brazil and Australia. Of course, the experiences of these women were diverse, rooted as they were in their cultural and social specificities. But what emerged from the discussion was the striking common element in their experiences as workers, especially in the treatment they received from the TNCs and from their male colleagues.[7] A woman from Hong Kong – Choi Wan Cheung – gave an account of the disillusionment of female workers during the Control Data hostilities in South Korea in 1981–2. During the strike staged by women operatives, male workers connived with the management and assumed a disciplinary role to keep women workers in their place. Exactly the same tactic was used by the Levi's company in Tennessee, said Corky Jennings, a union organizer of women workers in that state. Levi's used husbands, older brothers and fathers to oversee the women workers.

The feminist conference of women workers in the electronics, clothing and textiles industries on 24 April 1983 also represents a landmark in international solidarity of workers for transnational corporations. The conference was organized at County Hall in London by War on Want and the Archway Development Education Centre. It gave a forum to 170 women from the labour, trade union and women's movements from countries as far apart as Sri Lanka, Malaysia, the Philippines, Holland and Scotland. The analysis and discussion of the conditions of work in global companies at the conference clarified the role of TNCs in creating an unstable and vulnerable pattern of employment, be it in Malaysia or in Scotland. The exchange of information also confirmed the determination of workers to resist the divisive strategies of multinationals, that set black women against white and Third World women against First. The conference affirmed the need for establishing a continuous and powerful international network for disseminating information regarding conditions of work and resistance to the conditions imposed by TNCs. As a result of the conference, the now well-known network 'Women Working Worldwide' was set up.[8]

Apart from sharing the conviction that knowledge is power, women are increasingly becoming aware that togetherness is power. This new sense of solidarity brings female white-collar workers closer to their manual counterparts. The logic behind this solidarity is obvious: the twin effects of NT – automation and fragmentation – affect office and service work in the same way as manufacturing work. Flexi-workers in office jobs share the same

Japanese women organize

Computer drives out women
As if it were a friend of women
It drives out women

Computer is an enemy of women
Though it glitters and looks clean
It makes a woman cry

Oh computer,
Women have long been waiting for you,
Hoping that you help us to have more free time
And yet you, computer,
You have helped us to shed more tears

This short poem was written, in a notebook, like a murmur by a woman working at an office of an agricultural co-operative. The poem has become popular among Japanese workers for it expresses their own feeling while working at computerized offices.

Besides casualization of employment, the computerization affects women's health. It creates a new range of occupational diseases such as eyestrain caused by VDT work, sickness caused by low-level radiation from leaked VDT, shoulder-arm-neck syndrome caused by continuous work of VDT at the highest tension, mental disorder, excessive fatigue, all of which affect women.

. . . This is why we women workers have organized the Committee for Protection of Women in the Computer World. We hope that our movement to protect women's right to work will grow through learning from women workers' struggles in other countries.

Source: Committee for the Protection of Women in the Computer World, Japan's Women's Council, Tokyo, 1983.

vulnerability as casual workers on the factory floor, and the 'runaway' office jobs increasingly follow the well-trodden path of 'runaway' factory jobs. Awareness of this bond between manual and office workers brought together 60 women from the rich and the poor countries in Geneva on 19 June 1983, under the auspices of ISIS, a resource centre in the international women's liberation movement. The contributions of participants confirmed the need for increased solidarity to resist low wages and health hazards, that are often associated with NT in office work as well as in factory work. The discussions in fact successfully challenged the notion of NT as the liberator: the experiences of women workers confirmed that advances in technology had given a potent tool to management to intensify the work process. Hence it was agreed that there was a need to re-orient the labour movement to protect the interests of the growing number of low-paid workers and flexi-workers. Again an effective network was begun.[9]

The nascent parallel labour movement based on the exchange of information among women workers cannot afford to be blind to the racial dimension in the division of labour. Indeed, it would be unrealistic, in the name of womanly solidarity, to ignore the evidence of history. The distrust black women feel is voiced poignantly by Buchi Emecheta:

> Do you then blame us for being careful in following the white woman's footsteps? The blood of the black woman [for example] has helped so much in building the America of today; but look at her, living in poor areas of Palo Alto in California, look at her shacks in Sacramento, to say nothing of the east . . .[10]

The labour movement is also tarnished by its record of racism. The treatment of black workers by trade unions in the 1983 strike at the Peugeot-Talbot factories in France makes black women workers understandably cautious. Here the communist-led Confédération Générale du Travail (CGT) readily agreed to a redundancy plan that laid off mainly the black workers. This is particularly ironic as it is the struggle of Arab and North African workers in the Citroen-Aulney plant in 1982 that gave the CGT the strength it needed to gain organizational control from the 'yellow' union.[11]

The Imperial Typewriters strike, organized mainly by Asian men and women, in Leicester in 1974 also typifies the difficulty black workers face in identifying themselves with the white-dominated mainstream labour movement. The strike, which started as a protest against economic and racial exploitation, developed into 'an all-out battle against the management, the agencies of the state which attempted to mediate, and the Transport and General Workers' Union (TGWU), which denied support to the strikers and attempted to assist the management in defeating them'.[12]

In those cases where trade unions did come out in support of black women workers, the issue of race, if not of sex, became subsumed under the cause of defending the trade union movement. The Grunwick strike in 1977, one of the major and most publicized strikes of the 1970s, drew the support of white workers, who attended the mass pickets organized by the strike committee. Indeed, the Grunwick struggle soon became symbolic of the fundamental right of a worker to belong to a union. The fact that most of the strikers were Asian women was seen as 'incidental'. As Pratibha Parmar documents, this negation of the race and gender of the strikers was exemplified by one miner saying, 'We are right behind the lads here, they have our full support'.[13]

The need to be aware of the importance of racial issues, both in understanding the emerging structure of employment and in establishing bonds based on realistic awareness, was the guiding principle behind launching the third National Homeworking Conference. The conference was organized by the National Steering Group, an umbrella organization for UK-based homeworking campaign groups. It took place on 2 June 1984, at County Hall in London, and was attended by 150 participants from places ranging from Dundee to Amsterdam. The speakers highlighted the racist and sexist practices prevailing in society that give the TNCs easy access to the cheapest and most hidden type of labour in the form of homeworking. The participants, with justifiable humility, remembered the thousands of homeworkers who could not come to the conference. A woman from Lambeth said:

> We must not forget the number of women who are not in the conference today. They could not come because of racist and sexist practices, because they have no childcare, could not get on the trains (for lack of money) and could not come up to the microphone to speak (from fear of the authorities or lack of English).[14]

Homeworkers' charter

The demands contained in this Charter are those made by homeworkers. The vast majority are women who suffer the triple burdens of childcare, housework and paid employment. Homeworkers are caught in the poverty trap and as such provide cheap, unorganized labour, especially for the sectors of industry which perpetuate the worst employment practices. Homeworking, especially in the new technology industries, both in manufacturing and the provision of services, is on the increase; it is now being promoted as the way of working in the future even by multinational concerns. It is clear that the bad employment practices of traditional industries are being imported into the newer ones to the detriment of worker organization. Homeworkers, who are particularly vulnerable to racist and sexist exploitation, subsidize their employer's profits and there is no doubt that given better opportunities few homeworkers would work at home.

This Charter therefore demands that:

1. Free adequate care of dependants is available for homeworkers
A majority of homeworkers say that they are forced to work at home in order to look after children, or sick, elderly or disabled dependants, and that if adequate care were freely available this would enable them to work outside the home.

2. Resources are provided to enable homeworkers to meet together for mutual support, organization and campaigning
Homeworkers live and work in isolated conditions with little or no opportunity for exchanging information with each other, or for recreation. If homeworkers are to improve their economic status these resources must be made available.

3. Employee status is given to homeworkers
Lack of clarity about employment status of homeworkers has resulted not only in the casualization of homeworkers' labour but also in the loss of other rights and benefits which depend on proof of employment status: e.g., sick pay, Unemployment Benefit, Maternity Benefit, Family Income Supplement, pensions, etc. In addition, homeworkers subsidize their employer's business by paying rent, rates, heating, lighting, running and maintaining their machines. The employer also does not pay any staffing costs, thus avoiding capital and revenue outlay.

4. An end to racist and sexist practices and the repeal of racist and sexist legislation

The isolation and fear which homeworkers suffer are compounded by the laws, attitudes and practices of a society which is essentially racist and which denies the right of all women to participate socially and economically in it. Institutional racism and sexism informs the attitudes and procedures which exclude women and black and minority ethnic people from the benefits of the community to which they contribute.

5. The adoption of a national minimum wage

The adoption of a national minimum wage for all workers is essential in order to end the super-exploitation of homeworkers, people with disabilities and other unprotected groups. One national minimum wage will eliminate the problems associated with the complicated Wages Council Orders and their present lack of enforcement.

6. The amendment of relevant regulations to ensure that homeworkers and their families do not suffer injury, disease or sickness as a result of their work

Homeworkers use dangerous substances such as glues, fixes and solvents, unguarded machinery and VDUs in their home without the protection afforded all other workers. They carry the responsibility for the health and safety of themselves and their families which should by right be that of their employer. The Health and Safety at Work Act must be amended to include all homeworkers.

7. Comprehensive training and educational opportunities for homeworkers

Given the opportunity homeworkers prefer to work outside the home. Some lack the necessary skills and education to participate in the labour market; some are skilled in one process of production which may well be in a rapidly changing industry; some skilled workers may have been out of paid work while raising children and their skills need upgrading; some have never had the opportunity.

Source: Greater London Council, *The London Industrial Strategy*, 1985.

It was recognized particularly at this conference that institutional racism places black women at a special disadvantage. Faced with additional obstacles, black women at times feel that racism is more of an evil in their lives than sexism. An Asian woman from the Greenwich Homeworking Project voiced the dilemma:

> For many Asian and black women, there are greater problems than [the loneliness, health hazards and financial insecurity] associated with homeworking: there are racist attacks, being a single parent in an alien culture, and fear of immigration authorities.[15]

To challenge the racist element in the spread of homeworking, therefore, became a major objective in the Charter of Homeworking formulated by the Steering Group.

One of the important contributions of the feminist labour movement is that it seriously challenges the male-dominated, class-biased and Eurocentric vision of growth and development. The post-war flourishing academic discipline of 'Development Economics' was based on the unquestioned superiority of European societies.[16] The socio-economic maturity of a non-European nation was measured against a norm prevailing and accepted in white society. The ethos of international agencies reflected the nineteenth-century social Darwinism that viewed all non-European cultures simply as poorer versions of European civilization. Black societies were regarded as belonging to the childhood of mankind, whose maturity had been reached only in white societies. The desirability and the necessity of evolving one's own path of development, oriented towards a country's history, tradition and specific needs, were not seen as important. The concept of 'appropriate technology' was regarded as eccentric. In this intellectual milieu, TNCs were seen as welcome and universal levellers, as harbingers of modern and superior societies.

Similarly, in white societies the improvement of the working class was planned for them by the elite. The people were treated as a 'dull compendious mass', to borrow Thomas Carlyle's phrase, in the restructuring of the post-war economy. Bea Campbell describes the disastrous consequences of such attitudes in the context of housing policy:

> The municipal merchants of mass housing for the people planned homes *for* the people, not with them, they forced high-rise blocks, for example, on reluctant inhabitants. They knew people did not like them, but they built them nonetheless.[17]

The zeal of doing things for people rather than with people permeated left-wing political thinking as well. Bea Campbell recounts:

> A contemporary of mine once said, self-critically, 'I used to think that what I was fighting for was for the people to have access to a good education, good housing, good books, to be fearless, to be like me, actually.'[18]

Such condescension in planning, as well as the class-biased, neo-colonial policies of national and international agencies, are now being rejected by the grassroots feminist movements in favour of a more caring, sharing and co-operative economic structure. In the search for this, women in the West are looking for models to emulate in non-Western societies – models such as GABRIELA in the Philippines or the Self-Employed Women's Association (SEWA) in India. GABRIELA, as we have seen, is a movement of women workers who aim to restructure their society in order to use the nation's resources for the betterment of all its people. As a precondition of this goal, they wage a struggle to free the Philippines from the military and economic domination of foreign powers, especially of the United States. In addition, the movement provides the strength and inspiration behind a new type of unionism where both the leadership and the membership consist entirely of women workers.

The Kilusan Ng Manggagawang Kababaihan (KMK) is the Philippine Women Workers' Movement; a union since 1984, it is linked to Kilusan Mayo Uno (KMU), the 'May 1 Movement' of militant workers. KMU, organized clandestinely under martial law in 1980, is distinct from 'yellow unions' and includes both men and women. Women workers can be members of KMU as

The GABRIELA movement

GABRIELA, a National Women's Coalition of more than 70 organizations and institutions, is convening an international women's solidarity conference on March 7, 1986 as an important part of an eight-day program of women's activities and events called the Women's International Solidarity Affair in the Philippines, or WISAP, which will surround the celebration of the March 8 International Women's Day in our country. . . .

As the economic and political crisis in the Philippines heightens and women's oppression is intensified, GABRIELA recognizes the urgent need to build stronger bonds of solidarity with our friends and establish new solidarity links with women's organizations throughout the world and to learn from their experiences as they strive for women's empowerment and development in their own societies.

Source: GABRIELA, Metro Manila, Philippines, 17 October 1985.

well as of KMK. It is KMK that concentrates on the gender-specific issues, such as childcare, low pay, maternity leave, flexible working time – the kinds of issues that tend to get lost or diffused in a male-dominated trade union movement. This dual structure heralds an organizational innovation in trade unionism reflecting the communality as well as the divergences in the interests of men and women workers.

SEWA is also a trade union movement of a novel kind. Its membership consists of scattered, self-employed and home-based women workers, who constitute a major part of the female workforce in the famous textiles city of Ahmedabad, in the western province of India. Its 25,000-odd members are recruited from a variety of professions. The women in SEWA may be petty roadside vendors, rollers of 'Bidi' (indigenous cigarettes), basket-makers, or vegetable sellers. They represent the poorest and the most exploited sections of the community, and a great many of them are Harijans (untouchables). In some trades, nearly half of the women are the sole supporters of their family, as their men have either deserted or migrated in search of better jobs. Although potentially vulnerable, the lives and working

SEWA in India influences the strategies of home-working campaign groups in Europe

1. To ensure visibility –
   (a) by organizing them into units/co-operatives:
   (b) by giving publicity about their existence.
2. To wage a struggle – for better conditions for work and pay.
3. To involve women in development activities – by giving experience in banking, marketing and retailing.

From pressure to command

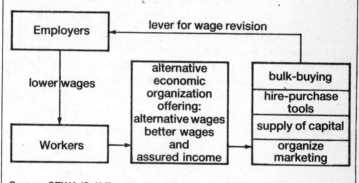

Source: SEWA (Self-Employed Women's Association), India.

conditions of these women have been transformed by this immensely successful union of self-employed women. SEWA – the acronym resembles the word that means 'service' in most Indian languages – was founded in 1972 and became an autonomous movement when it broke away from its parent organization, the Textiles Labour Association, in 1981. The split came about as a result of SEWA's taking up the cause of Harijans, in the outbreak of violence over the issue of positive discrimination in favour of this lowest of castes. All along, under the inspiring guidance of Ela Bhatt, SEWA has provided a constructive, rather than merely reactive, approach to the labour movement. In her words:

The purpose of trade unionism is not only for agitation. It is about solidarity and development: 89 per cent of women workers in Ahmedabad are self-employed. If they are excluded from the labour movement, you are cutting off the vast majority of workers, and those who most need protection.[19]

This broad vision of the labour movement can sustain itself only through the economic strength of its members. Hence SEWA arranges not only for upgrading the skills of its members in production, retailing, marketing, but also for giving them adequate access to finance. The most impressive achievement of SEWA to date has been to set up its own bank for its members, who are poor and mostly illiterate, and who cannot provide any collateral to an ordinary finance house. Based on the strength of the small savings of its members, SEWA can now boast a rate of default that is much lower than that in commercial banks.[20]

As the casualization of employment becomes all-pervasive in the West, the achievement of SEWA provides a model for organizing women workers in the advanced economies of Europe. Echoing the messages of Ela Bhatt, the women's movement in the West now also questions the present trend in the trade union movement that marginalizes the ever-growing number of casual and home-based workers.

Alternative economic strategies

Reversing this trend will imply recognizing a fresh definition of the working class. It will also necessitate, in the spirit of GABRIELA, a revaluation of the instruments as well as the goals of economic planning.

This new approach is as important for the mature West as it is for the newly emerging non-European countries. An awareness of this has led to formulations of a number of alternative strategies in Western Europe. The experiments with 'municipal socialism' under the labour-controlled Greater London Council (GLC) between 1981 and 1986 have been among the most comprehensive. In 1981 the GLC, under the leadership of Ken Livingstone, pledged its commitment to a new version of socialism.

Over the brief period of five years, it tried to build a participatory socialism, bringing together women, ethnic minorities and other new social forces. There was a fresh vision of economic renewal: the plan was to work towards the restructuring of labour, to borrow Robin Murray's phrase, rather than the restructuring of capital.[21]

In this brand of socialism, there was no reason to make the state the centre of power. Of course, a certain amount of state support was necessary, but only in so far as it increased the competitive power of labour. To what extent the experiment with municipal socialism was successful is for the historians to evaluate, but it definitely mobilized support from the general public on a scale that challenged the philosophy of the central, monetarist government, committed to its belief in free market mechanisms and the invigoration of international capital. The experiment had to be stopped. The abolition of the GLC by central government in March 1986 was itself a tribute to the success of the GLC's policies.

In case the experiment should simply disappear into the folk-history of London, the GLC in 1985 produced a document entitled *The London Industrial Strategy 1985 (LIS)*, to enable its strategy to obtain the serious consideration it deserved.[22] In it, the socialist GLC provided a coherent and detailed blueprint for an alternative economic strategy in the context of Greater London, based on some in-depth research on the main industrial sectors that generate employment for Londoners.

The radical new departure in *LIS* is that it acknowledges the crucial roles of domestic work and childcare in restructuring the local economy. By extending the social provision of caring, it promises to reverse the central government policy that 'is shifting work back into the household'.[23] This promise is particularly significant as the document explicitly relates the discrimination women face in paid jobs to the role of women at home. It is for this reason perhaps that *LIS*, uniquely among socialist blueprints, incorporates a chapter on the growth of homeworking. The GLC recognizes that this represents the logical outcome of the current restructuring of capital, which thrives on increased subcontracting and on the racial and sexual divisiveness among workers.

Increasing the competitiveness of workers in relation to monopoly capital is the aim of the GLC's strategy. In this connection, the production of goods and services plays a central role. The council's approach contrasts sharply with mainstream economic philosophy, embedded in monetarism and Keynesianism, both of which place undue emphasis on financial indicators relating to foreign exchange, the stock market, or the money supply. The establishment economists, obsessed with the money veil of the economy, have shown too little concern for the vital issues of people and production. As the *LIS* states:

> Thus, ignored by economists, production has been left as the province of the engineer, the production manager and the industrial relations consultant [who give] . . . overriding priority to private market production and to the military sector, and the technological replacement of awkward labour. We can call this *militarized market production*. It represents the economics of capital.

The alternative, therefore, is to work towards the economics of labour, where the planners aim to provide work for all those who wish it in jobs that are geared to meeting social needs. The role of technology, in such a scheme, is to reskill labour and thereby improve its competitiveness, rather than to deskill workers for the benefit of management.

The Greater London Enterprise Board (GLEB) was set up in 1983 precisely to augment this aim. It still exists, but with much reduced resources now that the GLC is gone. As a vital institution of the GLC, it provided assistance to create or save jobs in firms that offered better wages and greater control by workers, and manufactured socially useful goods. The principal aim of the Board was to evolve what Mike Cooley, the Director of GLEB, called a 'human-centred technology'. His commitment to promote this was based on the current feminist critique of science and technology. In his words:

> The prevailing technology reflects the economic base and power relations of the society which has given rise to it, and displays predominantly the value system of *the white male capitalist warrior hero*.[24]

To change this value system meant, therefore, to alter the power base itself and thereby the accepted social relations of production.

The GLC and GLEB fall somewhat short of offering the steps for achieving such an alteration. The promises of crèche facilities, of an expansion of social provisions, and of urging or forcing firms to be equal opportunity employers, are important but by no means sufficient steps for achieving gender equality at work. The *LIS* for example does not take up the issue of hours of work – a question that many feminist economists see as crucial to progress in achieving equality between genders.[25] Without a provision for shorter working hours and a more flexible pattern of employment, which would make it possible for the tasks involved in bringing up children to be shared, gender equality will be hard to achieve. By not stressing the importance of such a demand, therefore, even the *LIS* would seem to be building its socialist base on the accepted image of a woman who is or should be solely responsible for the caring jobs. As long as this assumption remains unchanged, it becomes difficult to make a dent in the myth of the male breadwinner – hitherto the crucial concept in constructing a role for women in the job market.

Again the *LIS*, representing an island of socialism in a market-oriented society, can pose only a limited challenge to the large corporations. The hope of counteracting the power of the global corporations is seen primarily in obtaining a deep knowledge of the interconnection between different sectors: 'the French refer to it as the *filière*, the thread of industrial organization'.[26] In the absence of such knowledge, however, the *LIS* states, 'public intervention itself may become in the end a mere support for those who control the commanding economic heights and who have themselves decentralized to subcontractors'.[27]

The knowledge itself can hardly alter the existing social relations of production unless we demand accountability regarding the corporations' sources of supply. The multinational retailers are precisely the ones that the *LIS* fears as commanding 'economic heights'. By accepting their power in the market, the *LIS* at times appears like a report written by 'radical management consultants',[28] helping the small and ailing firms in the inner city to win the custom of the big retailers.

Municipal socialism can be fully successful only with the support of central government. The political mobilization at the grassroots level can then be used to bring about the desired changes in the structure of the market as well as in the accepted social relations of production. In this future scenario, it may be possible to demand accountability from the flexible international companies, but only with the help of firsthand knowledge of the hierarchy of sub-contracting that links homeworkers and other vulnerable workers to the worldwide strategies of the multinationals.

The grassroots organizations of women workers, such as homeworking campaign groups in the UK, can offer precisely this vital knowledge regarding industrial organization that the re-structuring of labour requires. In London since 1981, such or-ganizations have been funded by the GLC, who have also provided the facilities for them to meet comparable groups from other countries. Thus, the strong links that are being forged among such organizations across national boundaries can provide the force for taking up the challenge of the multinationals internationally.

The growing awareness of the limited ability of nation-states to counteract the supranational powers of global corporations has already led to a visibly transnational approach in the socialist planning of West European countries. In the well-publicized manifesto, *Out of Crisis – A Project for European Recovery*, the need for a concerted European plan for a socialist expansionary policy of reflation, redistribution and restructuring has been stressed. The manifesto, known as the 'Alternative Economic Strategy' (AES), demands, in Stuart Holland's phrase, an end to 'beggar my neighbour' deflation, and the adoption of co-ordinated 'better my neighbour' expansionary policies.[29] Such a mechanism of European macro-management to replace national management seems particularly urgent when, to quote Ken Livingstone, 'Europe . . . is overcast by the shadow of the American economy just as it is overcast militarily by the shadow of the American arsenal.'[30] To change course is not going to be easy. It would involve, as Ken Coates argues, 'a new set of relationships with the Third World and with developing China. This would be a coalition for peace, as well as development and recovery.'[31] In particular this new internationalism, as Frances Morrell reminds us,

. . . is anti-Atlanticist. If it is to be carried through, then conflict with the current Presidency of the United States is inevitable. Equally inevitable is some conflict with major American and Japanese multinationals trading in Europe, with international financial institutions like IMF, and with the EEC over some of the clauses of the Treaty of Rome.[32]

Implementing a transnational socialist programme of recovery would involve the linking of the labour movement across Europe in a plan to enlist the explicit co-operation of the workers of the countries concerned. John Palmer envisages establishing such links through agitational campaigns for jobs and welfare rights by trade unions, following the model set by the European Nuclear Disarmament movement.[33]

In such a vision, however, the labour movement is being assigned only a reactive role.[34] At the same time, it implies a too facile identification of the labour movement with the mainstream trade union-based workers' movement. At the current stage of global industrial restructuring, when the growth area of employment is only in casualized jobs and home-based work, the strategy for participatory socialism is certain to founder unless it reckons with the co-operation of the grassroots organizations representing women and black workers.

It is on the basis of reasoned analysis, therefore, that the 'Alternative Economic Strategy' of the left is viewed by women and blacks as a manifesto written by white male activists, reflecting the traditions of the male-dominated labour movement. The agenda puts more emphasis on the manufacturing sector, which is viewed as the engine for growth, and less on the services which are the basis for distributive justice. Neither does the AES consider the arbitrariness in the definition of skills, and in the notion of a family wage – two factors that have been instrumental in subjecting women to the status of low-pay workers.[35]

If women feel marginalized in the European plan for socialist expansionary policy, so too do blacks. In a society where black families live in constant fear of violence and where black youth faces overt discrimination in jobs and training, socialism becomes an empty promise without a positive assurance of distributive justice.

Nor should such a strategy overlook the basic tenets of feminist socialism, that are rooted in a belief in the equality of gender as well as of class. It is imperative therefore that, in an alternative economic strategy, the household should be seen as a focal point and domestic work seen to play a vital role. As we have observed, the division between core male workers and peripheralized women workers in the international political economy is based precisely on the generally accepted role of women in the domestic sphere. Hence it will be futile to counteract the challenges of the global corporations until and unless there are extended social provisions for the care of the young and the elderly, and men are willing to share domestic work.

Finally, an alternative strategy needs to build its base on the ongoing socialist experiments at the community level. It is indeed only a community-based network that can effectively assess and harmonize economic, emotional and environmental needs. Through their campaigns for organizing homeworkers, flexi-workers and workers in the unregulated economy, feminist labour movements are offering different variants of such community networks. In spirit, their vision is akin to what Rudolf Bahro would have called a 'non-capitalist path of production'.[36] In the Lega delle Co-operative in Rome, Italian feminists have, for example, submitted such a blueprint of grassroots socialism. I cannot do better than quote them verbatim:

> Would it not be possible, for instance, to introduce a modernized version of the old practice whereby a housing co-operative would be regarded as being not only the group of people living in the same building, but also as the place where the services needed by these people are organized? And would it not be possible to encourage members of the producers' co-operatives to create ways of channelling company profits to benefit the community (in cultural, touristic, welfare and other activities)? Could consumers' co-operatives not come to an agreement with social services co-operatives to allow their members to have privileged rates for specific services? This would stimulate new experiments in the areas of social services, which then

would be assured of a stable market within the co-operative circuit. And women would benefit from this, since they would once again find an effective channel for voicing their collective needs: they would have a new – though at the same time a very old – weapon in their battle for emancipation and freedom.[37]

When such grassroots experiments gather momentum, one hopes that the mainstream labour movement will reach out to join the new yet already dynamic women workers' movement. A British trade union banner of the early twentieth century proclaimed:

> The world is my country,
> Mankind are my brethren,
> To do good one to another is my religion.[38]

The time has now come to make explicit room for womankind in these phrases if we are to build solidarity for employment and justice.

Notes

1. Women and the changing structure of employment

1 F. Fröbel, J. Heinrichs and O. Kreye, *The New International Division of Labour*, Cambridge: Cambridge University Press 1980.

2 Howard Rush and Kurt Hoffman, 'Microelectronics and the Clothing Industry' (unpublished), Brighton Polytechnic and Sussex University 1984, for obtaining figures for Western Europe and the United States. For the Third World, my own estimate from a number of sources.

3 Nigel Harris, *Of Bread and Guns: the World Economy in Crisis*, Harmondsworth: Penguin 1983, Chapter 5.

4 L. Taylor, 'Back to Basics', *World Development*, Vol. 10, No. 4, 1982.

5 Diane Elson, 'North–South Links Between Producers and Consumers', *Conference Documentation: Third World Trade and Technology Conference*, Vol. 1, London: Greater London Council and Twin Trading Ltd. 1985, p. 10.

6 R. Edwards, *Contested Terrain: The Transformation of the Workplace in the Twentieth Century*, London: Heinemann 1979, p. 8.

7 R.J. Barnet and R.E. Müller, *Global Reach*, London: Jonathan Cape 1975.

8 Cited in Teresa Hayter, *The Creation of World Poverty*, London: Pluto Press 1981, p. 104.

9 *Ibid.*, p. 104.

10 Rachael Grossman, 'Women's Place in the Integrated Circuit' in *Changing Role of South East Asian Women*, Southeast Asia Chronicle and Pacific Research, a Special Joint Issue, 1979, p. 11.

11 Antoine Basile and Dimitri Germidis, *Investing in Free Export Processing Zones*, Paris: OECD 1984, pp. 34–5.

12 L. Paukert, 'Personal Preference, Social Change or Economic Necessity: Why Women Work?', *Labour and Society*, Vol. 7, 1982.

13 Nigel Meager, *Temporary Work in Britain: Its Growth and Changing Rationales*, Sussex: Institute of Manpower Studies 1985.

14 Yut-Lin Wong, *Ghettoization of Women Workers in the Electronics Industry*, MPhil thesis at the Institute of Development Studies, University of Sussex, 1983.

Kevin Morgan and Andrew Sayer, 'A Modern Industry in a Mature

Region: the Re-making of Management Labour Relations', Working Paper 39, Urban and Regional Studies, University of Sussex, 1984.

15 Swasti Mitter, 'Industrial Restructuring and Manufacturing Homework: Immigrant Women in the UK Clothing Industry', *Capital and Class*, No. 27, Winter 1986.

16 Charles Babbage, *On the Economy of Machinery and Manufacturers* (1835), London: Cass 1968.

17 Andrew Ure, *The Philosophy of Manufacture, or an Exposition of the Scientific, Moral and Commercial Economy of the Factory System of Great Britain* (1835), London: Cass 1967. Frederick Winslow Taylor, *Scientific Management* (1903), London: Greenwood Press 1976.

18 Harry Braverman, *Labour and Monopoly Capital*, New York and London: Monthly Review Press 1974.

19 Fröbel, Heinrichs and Kreye, *The New International Division of Labour*.

2. Runaway capital

1 G. Arrighi and B.J. Silver, 'Working Class Culture, Organization and Protest' in Charles Bergquist (ed), *Labour in the Capitalist Economy*, London: Sage Publications 1984, p. 204.

2 R.J. Barnet and R.E. Müller, *Global Reach*, London: Jonathan Cape 1975, pp. 154 and 161.

3 Arrighi and Silver, 'Working Class Culture', pp. 200–14.

4 Nigel Harris, *Of Bread and Guns: The World Economy in Crisis*, Harmondsworth: Penguin 1983, p. 147.

5 Stephen Castles, Heather Booth and Tina Wallace, *Here For Good: Western Europe's New Ethnic Minorities*, London: Pluto Press 1984.

6 *The Roots of Racism*, London: Junius Publications 1985, p. 32.

7 Stephen Castles, 'Racism and Repatriation: Europe's Ethnic Minorities', in *World View, 1985*, London: Pluto Press 1985, pp. 181–8.

8 A. Sivanandan, *A Different Hunger: Writings on Black Resistance*, London: Pluto Press 1982, p. 23.

9 *Ibid.*, pp. 3-54.

10 Makoto Itoh, 'The Great World Crisis and Japanese Capitalism', *Capital and Class*, No. 21, Winter 1983, p. 53.

11 Annette Fuentes and Barbara Ehrenreich, *Women in the Global Factory*, New York: Institute for New Communications 1982, p. 15.

12 Teresa Hayter, *The Creation of World Poverty*, London: Pluto Press 1981, p. 114.

13 Walden Bello, David Kinley and Elaine Elinson, *Development Debacle: The World Bank in the Philippines*, San Francisco: Institute for Food and Development Policy 1982, p. 133.

14 Pasuk Phongpaichit, *From Peasant Girls to Bangkok Masseuses*,

Geneva: International Labour Office 1982, p. 72.

15 *Ibid.*, p. 73.

16 Walden Bello, *Development Debacle*, p. 68.

17 Diane Elson and Ruth Pearson, ' "Nimble Fingers Make Cheap Workers": An Analysis of Women's Employment in the Third World Export Manufacturing', *Feminist Review*, No. 7, 1980.

18 *International Labour Reports*, Issue 7, January–February 1985, p. 21.

19 G. Edgren, *Spearheads of Industrialization or Sweatshops in the Sun?: A Critical Appraisal of Labour Conditions in Asian Export Processing Zones*, Research Working Paper, restricted, Bangkok: ILO-ARTEP 1982.

20 A. Basile and D. Germidis, *Investing in Free Export Processing Zones*, Paris: OECD 1984, p. 20.

21 T. Takeo, introduction to *Free Trade Zones and Industrialization of Asia*, Special Issue, Tokyo: AMPO 1977, pp. 1-5.

22 Basile and Germidis, *Investing*, p. 57.

23 B. Taylor and M.E. Bond, *Mexican Border Industrialization*, Michigan State University Business Topics 1968, p. 38. Cited in María Patricia Fernández-Kelly, *For We Are Sold, I And My People: Women and Industry in Mexico's Frontier*, New York: State University of New York Press 1983, p. 27.

24 American Chamber of Commerce, 1970, p. 5.

25 B. Taylor and M.E. Bond, *Mexican Border Industrialization*.

26 Basile and Germidis, *Investing*, p. 33.

27 Linda Y.C. Lim, *Women Workers in Multinational Corporations: The Case of the Electronics Industry in Malaysia and Singapore*, Michigan Occasional Papers, No. IX, Fall 1978, p. 7.

28 Barbara Ehrenreich and Annette Fuentes 'Life on the Global Assembly Line', *Ms*, January 1981, pp. 58–9.

29 International Confederation of Free Trade Unions, *Trade Unions and the Transnationals: Information Bulletin*, Brussels, March 1983, p. 17.

30 Rachael Grossman, 'Women's Place in the Integrated Circuit' in *Changing Role of South East Asian Women*, Southeast Asian Chronicle and Pacific Research, Special Joint Issue, Vol. 9, 1979, p. 8.

31 Basile and Germidis, *Investing*, p. 35.

32 *Manufacturing Clothier*, November 1984

33 Fuentes and Ehrenreich, *Women in the Global Factory*, pp. 15–18.

34 *Ibid.*, p. 18.

35 Fernández-Kelly, *For We Are Sold*, p. 181.

36 Diane Elson and Ruth Pearson, ' "Nimble Fingers Make Cheap Workers" ': *Feminist Review*, No. 7, p. 93.

37 Fuentes and Ehrenreich, *Women in the Global Factory*, p. 22.

38 *Ibid.*, p. 19.

39 Linda Lim, *Women Workers in Multinational Corporations*.

40 Barnet and Müller, *Global Reach*, p. 345.

41 Fuentes and Ehrenreich, *Women in the Global Factory*, pp. 8–9.

42 M. Kei, 'South Korea: The Working Class in the Masan Export Processing Zone' in *Free Trade Zones and Industrialization of Asia*, pp. 67-70.

43 *Women Workers in Asia*, ISIS International Bulletin No. 10, Rome and Geneva 1978, p. 12.

44 International Confederation of Free Trade Unions, p. 21.

45 Scottish Education and Action for Development, *Electronics and Development: Scotland and Malaysia in the International Electronics Industry*, Edinburgh 1985, p. 10.

46 *Ibid.*, p. 10.

47 Basile and Germidis, *Investing*, p. 34.

48 F. Deyo, *Export Manufacturing and Labour: The Asian Case*, in Charles Bergquist, pp. 280–3.

49 Cynthia Enloe, 'Women Textile Workers in the Militarization of South East Asia', in June Nash and M.P. Fernández-Kelly (ed), *Women, Men and the International Division of Labour*, New York: State University of New York Press 1983, p. 417.

50 Cited from various sources in E. Eisold, 'Young Women Workers in Export Industries: The Case of Semiconductor Industry in Southeast Asia', Working Paper, Geneva: International Labour Organization 1984, pp. 54-5.

51 Cynthia Enloe, 'Textile Industry Exploits Women Workers', *Multinationals Monitor*, 1982.

52 Fuentes and Ehrenreich, *Women in the Global Factory*, p. 23.

53 Fernández-Kelly, *For We Are Sold*, p. 141.

54 'Why I Oppose Kisaeng Tours', in Kathleen Barry *et al* (eds), *International Feminism: Networking Against Female Sexual Slavery*, New York 1984, pp. 64-72.

55 *Ibid.*, p. 67.

56 Pasuk Phongpaichit, *From Peasant Girls*, p. 22.

57 A. Lin Neumann, 'Hospitality Girls in the Philippines', in *Changing Role of South East Asian Women*, p. 18.

58 *Changing Role of South East Asian Women*, p. 18.

59 *Tourism and Prostitution*, ISIS International Bulletin No. 13, Geneva, 1979.

60 Kathleen Barry *et al* (eds), *International Feminism*, p. 125.

61 ISIS, also cited in Khin Thitsa, *Providence and Prostitution: Image and Reality for Women in Buddhist Thailand*, London: Change International Reports on Women and Society, 1980.

62 Basile and Germidis, *Investing*, p. 50.

63 The *Financial Times*, 15 May 1985, p. IV.

64 *International Labour Report*, Issue 10, July/August 1985, p. 14.

65 International Confederation of Free Trade Unions, p. 12.

66 Basile and Germidis, *Investing*, p. 49.

67 Teresa Hayter and Catherine Watson, *Aid: Rhetoric and Reality*, London: Pluto Press 1985, p. 22.

68 *Ibid.*, chapter 2.

69 'Poor Gets Poorer in Brazil as IMF Discusses Terms', *Financial Times*, 11 June 1982.

70 Hayter and Watson, *Aid*, p. 21.

71 Cardinal Paulo Evaristo Arns, 'The Destabilizing Poverty Crisis', paper presented at the 18th World Conference, Rome, Society for International Development, July 1985.

72 Hayter and Watson, *Aid*, p. 29.

73 Arns, *op. cit.*, p. 4.

74 Walden Bello, *Development Debacle*, p. 162.

75 Cited in Fuentes and Ehrenreich, *Women in t e Global Factory*, p. 41.

76 Interview with Swasti Mitter, March 1986, Brighton.

77 Cynthia Enloe, *Multinational Monitor*.

78 Christian Conference of Asia, *The Plight of Asian Workers in Electronics*, Hong Kong: Christian Conference of Asia – Urban Rural Mission, October 1982.

79 'We Can Fight', *International Labour Reports*, Issue 10, July-August 1985, pp. 13–17.

80 *Ibid*.

81 Literature from the GABRIELA movement, San Juan, Metro Manila, the Philippines.

82 *Ibid*.

3. The capital comes home

1 Michael McKignay, 'The Place of Multinational Companies in Ireland', 1984 (unpublished dissertation).

2 International Confederation of Free Trade Unions, *Trade Unions and the Transnationals*, Brussels 1983, pp. 5–7.

3 Adam Smith Institute, *Proposal for the Establishment of Freeports in the UK*, London 1981, p. 3.

4 E. Butler and M. Pirie, *Freeports*, London: Adam Smith Institute 1983, p. 21.

5 *Financial Times*, 4 August 1982. Cited in Fergus Murray, 'The Decentralization of Production – The Decline of the Mass-Collective Worker', *Capital and Class*, No. 19, Spring 1983.

Section I

1 Peter Murray and James Wickham, 'Technocratic Ideology and the Reproduction of Inequality: The Case of the Electronics Industry in the Republic of Ireland', in Graham Day *et al* (eds), *Diversity and Decomposition in the Labour Market*, London: Gower 1982, p. 182.

2 Scottish Education and Action For Development (SEAD), *Electronics and Development: Scotland and Malaysia in the International Electronics Industry*, p. 22.

3 Kevin Morgan and Andrew Sayer, *The International Electronics Industry and Regional Development in Britain*, Urban and Regional Studies, University of Sussex, Working Paper 34, p. 46.

4 The *Financial Times*, Special Report, 1 March 1985.

5 SEAD, *op. cit.*

6 *Ibid.*, p. 19.

7 Kevin Morgan and Andrew Sayer, Working Paper 34, p. 44.

8 Murray and Wickham, *Technocratic Ideology*, p. 185.

9 The *Sunday Times*, 27 May 1984.

10 The *Guardian*, 23 July 1985.

11 Murray and Wickham, *Technocratic Ideology* and Morgan and Sayer, *The International Electronics Industry*.

12 Morgan and Sayer, Working Paper 34, p. 48.

13 SEAD, *Electronics and Development*, p. 24.

14 *Ibid.*, p. 21.

15 The *Sunday Times*, 27 May 1984.

16 A. Phillips and B. Taylor, 'Sex and Skill: Notes Towards A Feminist Economics', *Feminist Review*, No. 6, 1980, p. 86.

17 Morgan and Sayer, *A 'Modern' Industry in a 'Mature' Region*, Working Paper No. 39, p. 10.

18 Cited *ibid*.

19 SEAD, *Electronics and Development*, p. 21.

20 Yut-Lin Wong, 'Ghettoization of Women Workers in the Electronics Industry', MPhil dissertation at the Institute of Development Studies at Sussex University (unpublished), p. 92.

21 E. Breitenbach, *Women Workers in Scotland*, Glasgow: Pressgang 1982 and cited in Yut-Lin Wong, *ibid*.

22 Cynthia Cockburn, *Brothers: Male Dominance and Technological Change*, London: Pluto Press 1983, p. 154. Yut-Lin Wong, 'Ghettoization', pp. 104–5.

23 See Ruth Pearson, 'Multinational Companies and the Female Labour Force in the Third and the First World: The Same Sides of Different Coins', Discussion Paper No. 159, School of Development Studies, University of East Anglia, May 1984, p. 19.

24 For a detailed analysis of the sexual composition of the labour force

see Ruth Pearson, 'The Greening of Women's Labour: Multinational Companies and Their Female Workforce in the Third and the First World', in K. Purcell *et al* (ed), *The Changing Experience of Employment*, London: Macmillan 1986.

25 Morgan and Sayer, Working Paper 34, p. 50.

26 Morgan and Sayer, Working Paper 39, p. 23.

27 Scottish Development Agency, *Labour Performance of US Plants in Scotland*, 1984, p. 11.

28 Yut-Lin Wong, 'Ghettoization', p. 66.

29 Roger Smith and John Humphrey, 'Quality Circles', *International Labour Reports*, Vol. 8, March–April 1985.

30 Morgan and Sayer, Working Paper 34, p. 60.

31 Scottish Development Agency, *Labour Performance in US Plants*, 1981, p. 12.

32 Stuart Howard, 'The UK No-strike Agreements – New Realism or Company Unionism?', *International Labour Reports*, Vol. 4, July–August 1984, p. 12.

33 *Ibid*.

34 *Ibid*.

35 Morgan and Sayer, Working Paper 34, p. 53.

36 Morgan and Sayer, Working Paper 39, pp. 18–22.

37 Nance Goldstein, 'The Women Left Behind: Technological Changes and Restructuring in the Electronics Industry in Scotland', paper presented at the workshop on 'Women and Multinationals in Europe', School of Development Studies, University of East Anglia, 1984. Cited in Ruth Pearson (see notes 23 and 24 above).

38 John Bessant and Bill Haywood, 'Tailor Your Flexible System to Suit Your Demands', *Works Management*, November 1985, p. 69.

Section II

1 John Atkinson, *Flexibility, Uncertainty and Manpower Planning*, Sussex: Institute of Manpower Studies, Report No. 89, 1984.

2 The *Sunday Times*, 22 April 1984.

3 Alan Bollard, 'Technology, Economic Change and Small Firms', *Lloyds Bank Review*, January 1983.

4 Fergus Murray, 'The Decentralization of Production – The Decline of the Mass-collective Worker', *Capital and Class*, No. 19, Spring 1983, p. 81.

5 Jeremy Boissevain, 'Small Entrepreneurs in Contemporary Europe', in R. Ward and R. Jenkins (eds), *Ethnic Communities in Business*, Cambridge: Cambridge University Press 1984.

6 Graham Bannock, 'The Clearing Banks and Small Firms', *Lloyds Bank Review*, October 1981.

7 *The London Industrial Strategy*, London: Greater London Council 1983, p. 34.

8 Quoted in Philip Mattera, 'Small is Not Beautiful: Decentralized Production and the Underground Economy in Italy', *Radical America*, Vol. 14, No. 5, 1980.

9 Robin Murray, *Economic Policy Report*, London: Greater London Council 1983, pp. 15–16.

10 Philip Mattera, *Off The Books: The Rise of the Underground Economy*, London: Pluto Press 1985, chapters 1 and 2.

11 Fergus Murray, 'The Decentralization of Production', p. 83.

12 The *Financial Times*, 'Special Report on Italy', 26 March 1984.

13 Fergus Murray, 'The Decentralization of Production', p. 92.

14 Alan Bollard, 'Technology, Economic Change and Small Firms'.

15 Philip Mattera, *Radical America*, p. 68.

16 Fergus Murray, 'The Decentralization of Production', p. 92.

17 J. Buxton, 'The Man Who Fashioned a Clothing Empire', the *Financial Times*, 24 October 1983. J. Withers and A. Fawcett, 'Family That Fashioned Universal Flair', *The Times*, 24 August 1984.

18 *Ibid.*, 1983.

19 *Ibid.*, 1984.

20 *Ibid.*, 1983.

21 Philip Mattera, *Radical America*, p. 68.

22 Fergus Murray, The Decentralization of Production', p. 79.

23 *Electronic Times*, 9 October 1980.

24 Naomi Katz and David S. Kemnitzer, 'Fast Forward: The Internationalization of Silicon Valley', p. 333, in June Nash and Maria Patricia Fernández-Kelly (eds), *Women, Men and the International Division of Labour*, New York: State University of New York Press 1983.

25 Saskia Sassen-Koob, 'Labour Migration and The New International Division of Labour', p. 194 in Nash and Fernández-Kelly, *ibid*.

26 The *Guardian*, 16 March 1985.

27 Annette Fuentes and Barbara Ehrenreich, *Women In The Global Factory*, New York: Institute For New Communications 1982, p. 50.

28 Catherine Hakim, 'Homework and Outwork: National Estimates From Two Surveys', *Employment Gazette*, January 1984, p. 10.

29 *Outworkers' Own*, Issue 2, March 1984, p. 2.

30 Sheila Allen, 'Production and Reproduction: The Lives of Women Homeworkers', *Sociological Review*, November 1983, p. 661.

31 *Ibid.*, p. 660.

32 Anneke Van Luijken, *Thuiswerk*, Bijlage, *Vrij, Netherlands,* 1 October 1983.

33 Jeremy Boissevain, 'Small Entrepreneurs in Contemporary Europe'.

34 Patrick Duffy, *Bengali Action Research Project, Tower Hamlets* (a background paper for the Commission of Racial Equality), 1979, unpublished.

35 Barbara Hoel, 'Contemporary Clothing Sweatshops' in *Work, Women and the Labour Market*, edited by Jackie West, London: Routledge Kegan Paul, 1982, p. 86.

36 Floya Anthias, 'Sexual Divisions and Ethnic Adaptation: The Case of Greek-Cypriot Women', in Annie Phizacklea (ed), *One Way Ticket: Migration and Female Labour*, London: Routledge & Kegan Paul 1984. S. Ladbury, 'Choice, Chance or No Alternative: Turkish Cypriots in Business in London', in R. Ward and R. Jenkins (eds) *op. cit.*

37 *Outworkers' Own*, Issue 6, 1982, p. 3.

38 *Below the Minimum: Low Wages in the Clothing Trade*, West Midlands Low Pay Unit, 1984.

39 *International Herald Tribune*, 1 September 1980.

40 *Manufacturing Clothier*, April 1981, p. 17.

41 Kurt Hoffman and Howard Rush, *Microelectronics and Clothing*, Science Policy Research Unit, Sussex University, 1985. Howard Rush and L. Soete, 'Clothing' in K. Guy (ed) *Technological Trends and Employment: Basic Consumer Goods*, London: Gower 1984.

42 The *Guardian*, 24 October 1984.

43 A.F. Raine, 'Combined and Uneven Development in the Clothing Industry: The Effects of Competition on Accumulation', *Capital and Class*, No. 22, Spring 1984.

44 *Guardian*, 7 November 1983.

45 *The Times*, 28 October 1983.

46 Swasti Mitter, 'Industrial Restructuring and Manufacturing Homework: Immigrant Women in the UK Clothing Industry', *Capital and Class*, No. 27, Winter 1986.

47 Ursula Huws, 'New Technology Homeworkers', *Employment Gazette*, January 1984, p. 14.

48 *Business Week*, 26 January 1981.

49 Phil Judkins and David West, 'A Case History: Rank Xerox' in *Flexible Manning – The Way Ahead*, Institute of Manpower Studies, University of Sussex, Report No. 88, 1984, p. 17 (paraphrased).

50 Ursula Huws, 'New Technology Homeworkers', p. 17.

51 Ursula Huws, *The New Homeworkers: New Technology and the Changing Location of White Collar Workers*, London: Low Pay Unit 1984, p. 43.

52 Elsbeth Monod, 'Le Télétravail: Une nouvelle manière de travailler', *Datafrance*, 15 September 1983.

53 Ursula Huws, 'The Runaway Office Jobs', *International Labour Reports*, Vol. 2, March–April 1984, p. 10.

54 *Ibid*.

4. Women working worldwide

1 André Gorz, *Farewell to the Working Class: An Essay on Post-Industrial Socialism*, London: Pluto Press 1982, pp. 10–11.
2 *Ibid.*, p. 143.
3 *Ibid.*, p. 82.
4 Ivan Illich, *Gender*, London: Marion Boyers Publishers 1983, p. 66.
5 *Ibid.*, p. 57.
6 *Ibid.*, p. 60.
7 Wendy Chapkis and Cynthia Enloe (eds), *Of Common Cloth, Women In the Global Textiles Industry*, Amsterdam: Transnational Institute, and London: Pluto Press 1983.
8 *Women Working Worldwide: The International Division of Labour in the Electronics, Clothing and Textiles Industries*, London: War On Want, and Wiser Links 1983.
9 ISIS, *International Women and New Technology Conference*, Women's International Bulletin, Geneva, No. 28, 1983.
10 Buchi Emecheta, 'White Sisters Listen', *New Internationalist*, August 1985, p. 19.
11 'The Battle of Peugeot Talbot', *International Labour Reports*, Issue 2, March–April 1984.
12 Pratibha Parmar, 'Gender, Race and Class: Asian Women In Resistance', in *The Empire Strikes Back: Race and Racism in 70s Britain*, London: Hutchinson 1982, p. 264.
13 Quoted in *Spare Rib*, No. 66 and documented in Pratibha Parmar, 'Gender, Race and Class, p. 267.
14 Greater London Council, *Report of the National Homeworking Conference of 1984*, London, 1986.
15 *Ibid.*
16 Partha Mitter, 'Should Artificial Intelligence Take Culture Into Consideration?' in K.S. Gill (ed), *Artificial Intelligence For Society*, London: John Wiley 1986.
17 Beatrix Campbell, *Wigan Pier Revisited: Poverty and Politics in the 80s*, London: Virago Press 1984, p. 232.
18 *Ibid.*, p. 232.
19 Jeremy Seabrook, 'Sewa Plants The Seeds of Women's Rights', the *Guardian*, 12 April 1985, p. 14.
20 Self-Employed Women's Association (SEWA), *We, The Self Employed: Voice of The Self Employed Workers*, Ahmedabad, 1983.
21 Robin Murray, 'Pension Funds and Local Authority Investments', *Capital and Class*, No. 20, Summer 1983, p. 103.
22 Greater London Council, *The London Industrial Strategy, 1985*, London 1985, pp. 17–18.
23 *Ibid.*, p. 22.

24 *Computing*, 10 October 1980, p. 16.

25 Anne Phillips, *Hidden Hands: Women and Economic Policies*, London: Pluto Press 1984, chapter 4.

26 *The London Industrial Strategy, 1985*, p. 40.

27 *Ibid*.

28 Allan Cochrane, 'What's in a strategy? The London Industrial Strategy and Municipal Socialism', *Capital and Class*, No. 28, Spring 1986.

29 Stuart Holland (ed), *Out of Crisis: A Project For European Recovery*, Nottingham: Spokesman 1983.

30 Report to the Greater London Council, May 1984 and, in Ken Coates, 'A New Internationalism', *New Socialist*, September 1985, p. 38.

31 Ken Coates, *ibid*.

32 Frances Morrell, 'AES: The Alternative European Strategy', *New Socialist*, October 1985, p. 9.

33 John Palmer, 'New Vision of a Socialist Europe', *New Socialist*, No. 9, 1983, pp. 15–19.

34 Paul Teague, 'The Alternative Economic Strategy: A Time to Go European', *Capital and Class*, No. 26, Summer 1985, pp. 58–69.

35 Beatrix Campbell, 'Women: Not What They Bargained For', *Marxism Today*, March 1982.

36 Rudolf Bahro, *The Alternative in Eastern Europe*, London: New Left Books and Verso Editions, 1978.

37 Marta Nicolini, 'Idea: Investiamo nei servizi', *Noidonne*, November, 1982.

38 Quoted from *New Internationalist*, November 1982, p. 7.

A select bibliography

Allen, Sheila, 'Production and Reproduction: The Lives of Women Homeworkers', *Sociological Review*, November 1983.

Atkinson, John, *Flexibility, Uncertainty and Manpower Management*, Institute of Manpower Studies, Sussex University. Report No. 89, 1984.

Barnet, R.J. and R.E. Müller, *Global Reach: The Power of The Multinational Corporations*, London: Jonathan Cape 1975.

Barry, Kathleen *et al* (eds), *International Feminism: Networking Against Female Sexual Slavery*, 1984.

Bello, Walden, David Kinley and Elaine Elinson, *Development Debacle: The World Bank in the Philippines*, San Francisco: Institute for Food and Development Policy 1982.

Ben Jelloun, Tahar, *Hospitalité Française*, Paris: Seuil, 1984.

Campbell, Beatrix, 'Women: Not What They Bargained For', *Marxism Today*, March 1982.

Campbell, Beatrix, *Wigan Pier Revisited*, London: Virago Press 1984.

Castles, Stephen, Heather Booth and Tina Wallace, *Here For Good: Western Europe's New Ethnic Minorities*, London: Pluto Press 1984.

Centre for Contemporary Cultural Studies, *The Empire Strikes Back: Race and Racism in 70s Britain*, University of Birmingham 1982.

Chapkis, Wendy and Cynthia Enloe (eds), *Of Common Cloth: Women in the Global Textiles Industry*, Amsterdam: Transnational Institute 1983.

Christian Conference of Asia, *The Plight of Asian Workers in Electronics*, Hong Kong: Christian Conference of Asia – Urban Rural Mission, October 1982.

Cockburn, Cynthia, *Brothers: Male Dominance and Technological Change*, London: Pluto Press 1983.

Coote, Anna and Beatrix Campbell, *Sweet Freedom: A Struggle For Women's Liberation*, London: Pan Books 1982.

Elson, Diane and Ruth Pearson, ' "Nimble Fingers Make Cheap Workers": An Analysis of Women's Employment in the Third World', *Feminist Review*, No. 7, 1981.

Fernández-Kelly, Maria Patricia, *For We are Sold, I and My People. Women and Industry in Mexico's Frontiers*, New York: State University of New York Press, 1983.

Fröbel, F., J. Heinrichs and O. Kreye, *The New International Division of Labour*, Cambridge: Cambridge University Press 1980.

Fuentes, Annette and Barbara Ehrenreich, *Women in the Global Factory*, New York: Institute for New Communications 1982.

Gorz, André, *Farewell to the Working Class: An Essay on Post-Industrial Socialism*, London: Pluto Press 1982.

Greater London Council, *The London Industrial Strategy, 1985*, London: The GLC 1985.

Hakim, Catherine, 'Homework and Outwork: National Estimates From Two Surveys', *Employment Gazette*, January 1984.

Harris, Nigel, *Of Bread and Guns: The World Economy in Crisis*, Harmondsworth: Penguin 1983.

Hayter, Teresa, and Catherine Watson, *Aid: Rhetoric and Reality*, London: Pluto Press 1985.

Howard, Stuart, 'The UK No-strike Agreement – New Realism or Company Unionism?' *International Labour Reports*, July–August 1984.

Huws, Ursula, *The New Homeworkers: New Technology and the Changing Location of White Collar Workers*, London: Low Pay Unit 1984.

Illich, Ivan, *Gender*, London: Marion Boyes Publishers 1983.

ISIS, *International Women and New Technology Conference*, Geneva, No. 28, 1983.

Mattera, Philip, *Off The Books: The Rise of the Underground Economy*, London: Pluto Press 1985.

Mitter, Swasti, 'Industrial Restructuring and Manufacturing Homework', *Capital and Class*, No. 27, Winter 1986.

Monod, Elsbeth, 'Le Télétravail: Une nouvelle manière de travailler', *Datafrance*, 15 September 1983.

Morgan, Kevin and Andrew Sayer, *The International Electronics Industry and Regional Development in Britain*, Urban and Regional Studies, University of Sussex, Working Paper No. 34.

Murray, Fergus, 'The Decentralization of Production: The Decline of the Mass-Collective Worker', *Capital and Class*, No. 19, Spring 1983.

Murray, Peter and James Wickham, 'Technocratic Ideology and the Reproduction of Inequality: The Case of the Electronics Industry in the Republic of Ireland' in Graham Day *et al* (eds), *Diversity and Decomposition in the Labour Market*, London: Gower 1982.

Nash, June and Maria Patricia Fernández-Kelly (eds), *Women, Men and the International Division of Labour*, New York: State University of New York Press 1983.

Pearson, Ruth, 'The Greening of Women's Labour: Multinational Companies and Their Female Workforce in the Third and in the First World' in K. Purcell (ed), *The Changing Experience of Em-*

ployment, London: Macmillan 1986.

Phillips, Anne, *Hidden Hands: Women and Economic Policies*, London: Pluto Press 1983.

Phizacklea, Annie (ed), *One Way Ticket: Migration and Female Labour*, London: Routledge & Kegan Paul 1984.

Scottish Education and Action For Development (SEAD), *Electronics and Development: Scotland and Malaysia in the International Electronics Industry*, Edinburgh, 1985.

Sivanandan, A., *A Different Hunger*, London: Pluto Press 1982.

Southeast Asia Chronicle and Pacific Research, *Changing Role of South East Asian Women*, a special joint issue, 1979.

Thista, Khin, *Providence and Prostitution: Image and Reality for Women in Buddhist Thailand*, London: Change 1980.

Van Putten, Maartje and Nicole Lucas, *Made in Heaven: Women in the International Division of Labour*, Amsterdam: Evert Vermeer Stichting 1985.

Ward, R. and R. Jenkins (eds), *Ethnic Communities in Business*, Cambridge: Cambridge University Press 1984.

Women Working Worldwide, *The International Division of Labour in the Electronics, Clothing and Textiles Industry*, London: War on Want 1983.

Networking of women workers:
a select list of organizations involved in Europe

IRENE (Industrial Restructuring and Educational Network)
Korvelsweg 127
5025 JC Tilburg
The Netherlands
Tel: 013-433346

ISIS Italy
Via S. Maria dell' Anima 30
Rome
Italy
Tel: 06/656 58 42

ISIS Switzerland.
PO Box 50 Cornavain
1211 Geneva 2
Switzerland
Tel: 022/33 67 46

The National Group on Homeworking
132 Regent Road
Leicester LE1 7PA

National Women's Network For Worldwide Solidarity
22 Coleman Fields
London N1 7AG
Tel: 01-226 6616

The Philippines Support Group
PO Box 758
London WC1N 3XX

Tower Hamlets International Solidarity Group
Oxford House
Derbyshire Street
London E2
Tel: 01-739 9001

Transnationals Information Centre
9 Poland Street
London W1V 3DG
Tel: 01-734 5902

Transnational Information Exchange: Europe (TIE)
Transnational Institute
Paulus Potterstrat 20
1071 DA Amsterdam
The Netherlands

Twin Trading Limited (GLEB)
345 Goswell Road
London EC1

Wiser Links
173 Archway Road
London N6
Tel: 01-341 4403

Women Working Worldwide
War on Want
1 London Bridge Street
London SE1 9SG
Tel: 01-403 2266

Index